AutoCAD 2017
Training Guide

LINKAN SAGAR

BPB PUBLICATIONS

Distributors:

COMPUTER BOOK CENTRE
12, Shrungar Shopping Centre,
M.G.Road, BENGALURU–560001
Ph: 25587923/25584641

MICRO BOOKS
Shanti Niketan Building,
8, Camac Street, KOLKATA-700017
Ph: 22826518/22826519

DECCAN AGENCIES
4-3-329, Bank Street,
Hyderabad-500195
Ph: 24756967/24756400

MICRO MEDIA
Shop No. 5, Mahendra Chambers,
150 DN Rd. Next to Capital Cinema,
V.T. (C.S.T.) Station, MUMBAI-400 001
Ph: 22078296/22078297

BPB BOOK CENTRE
376 Old Lajpat Rai Market,
Delhi-110006
Ph: 23861747

INFOTECH
G-2, Sidhartha Building,
96, Nehru Place,
New Delhi -110019
Ph: 41619735, 26438245

BPB PUBLICATIONS
20, Ansari Road, Darya Ganj
New Delhi-110002
Ph: 23254990/23254991

Published by Manish Jain for BPB Publications, 20, Ansari Road, Darya Ganj, New Delhi- 110002 and Printed him at Akash Press, New Delhi.

Table of Contents

Preface

My vigorous effort towards the understanding of students & their problems in AutoCAD will probably solve after my attempt for this book.

So far my last book 'AUTOCAD 2015 REFERENCE' has been a success for my beloved readers. I have tried to be more eloquent this time with better projects easy language.

This book carries a lot for you if you are starting AutoCAD for the 1st time. Book is extremely simple to understand and can enlighten you with the basics fundamentals of AutoCAD.

The main objective of writing this book after getting inspired from my last edition is to make students enthusiastic about learning the concepts of AutoCAD.

I wish you a great future in designing.

"DESIGNING THE WORLD"

AutoCAD 2016 Beginning and Intermediate

ISBN:978-81-8333-585-0

₹ 594/-   Pages 788

This book is the most comprehensive book you will find on AutoCAD 2016-2D Drafting. Covering all of the 2D concept, it uses both metric and imperial units ti illustrate the myriad drawing and editing tools for this popular application. Use the CD to set up drawing exercises and projects and to see all of the intermediate includes over 100"mini-workshop" that complete small projects from concept through actual plotting. Solving all of these workshops will simulate to creation of three projects (architectural and mechanical) from beginning of end, without overlooking any of the basic commands and function in AutoCAD 2016.

FEATURES
✓ Designed for novice users of AutoCAD2016. Most useful for "teach yourself" or instructor-led AutoCAD training in level 1 or 2.
✓ Accompanied by a CD featuring drawing, practice and finished plot, 4-colors figures, etc.
✓ Includes over 100 "mini-workshop"and hundreds of figure that complete small projects.
✓ Uses both English and metric units in example, exercises, projects.
✓ Cover three full projects (metric and imperial)for architectural and mechanical designs.
✓ Helps you to prepare for the AutoCAD Certified Professional exam.

BRIEF TABLE OF CONTENTS
✓ AutoCAD216 Basics
✓ Precise Drafting In AutoCAD 2016
✓ Modifying Commands Part 1
✓ Modifying Commands Part 2
✓ Layer and Inquiry Commands
✓ Block and Hatches
✓ Writing Text
✓ Dimensions
✓ plotting
✓ Project
✓ More on 2D Objects
✓ Advanced Practices- part 1
✓ Advanced Practices- Part 2
✓ Using Block and Tools and block Editing
✓ Creating Text, Table Style, And Formula In Table Style
✓ Dimension & Multileader Style
✓ Plot Style, Annotative, And Exporting
✓ How To Create A Template File And
✓ Interface Customization
✓ Parametric Constraints
✓ Dynamic Blocks
✓ Block Attributes
✓ External Referencing (XREF)
✓ Sheet Sets
✓ Cad Standards & Advanced Layers
✓ Drawing Review

AutoCAD 2016 3D Modeling

ISBN: 978-81-8333-586-7

₹ 397/-   Pages 409

This book provides new and seasoned users with step by step procedures on creating and modifying 3D models, working with cameras and lights, assigning to objects, rendering, and printing. Unlike many AutoCAD competitors, it uses both metric and imperial units to illustrate the myriad tools for this popular application. Use the companion disc to set up drawing exercises and projects and see all of the book's figures including color. AutoCAD 2016 3D Modeling includes 50 "Miniworkshops" that complete small projects form concepts through actual projects (architectural and mechanical) from beginning to end, without overlooking any of the basic commands and functions in AutoCAD 2016.

FEATURES
− Covers 3D solid modeling surface modeling, working with cameras/lighting, rendering and imaging, dimensioning and drafting and model interchange
− Includes 50 "mimi-workshops" that complete small projects from concept through actual plotting. Solving all of the workshops will simulate the creation of full projects (architectural and mechanical)
− Provides new and seasoned suers with step by step procedures on creating and modifying 3D models in both metric and imperial units
− Companion disc can be used to set up in-text drawing exercises and projects and to see the book's figures in color
− Written by an AutoDesk Approved instructor and certified AutoDesk AutoCAD Master

BRIEF TABLE OF CONTENTS
− AutoCAD 2016 3D Basics
− Creating solid
− Creating Meshes
− Creating Surfaces
− Creating Complex Solid & Surfaces
− Solid Editing Commands
− 3D Modifying Commands
− Converting And Sectioning
− Printing In 3D And Creating 3D DWF Files
− Cameras And Lights
− Materials, Rendering, Visual Style And Animation

Acknowledgements

While writing this book, I was constantly supported and guided by many wonderful people around me. Their extended support will always be priceless for me. My mother Mrs. Archana Sagar, is a woman of Substance. Like any other mother in the world, her unconditional support, caring nature, never ending Faith in me, and motivation encouraged me to finally realize that I can transfer my knowledge through writing to various other people who seek the same knowledge. And this is how my book writing started.

Many thanks to my wife Mansi sagar, who is a wonderful partner, she not only understands my dreams and aspirations but is equally trying to internalize and live it up with me. Its wonderful how she took all the responsibilities on her own shoulder to give me space and comfort so that I can dedicate more time for writing. She stands strong with me in all the highs and lows of my life. These two women are the source of continuous energy that keeps me going.

My book is all about technical skills precision and perfection in the engineering field, I am highly obliged to My Mentor Mr. Abhishek Kaushik, for his guidance in Design Approvals throughout my writing, His sharp technical & analytical skills and in-depth knowledge of the subject matter, amazed me. It is due to his continuous guidance I could write a book of relevance and great content.

I am equally thankful to Ms. Nivedita Chaudhary, who took the responsibility of proof reading my writing and editing to make it grammatically sound and graspable. Her expertise and great insight helped a lot in shaping my book contents and put my thoughts in appropriate words. My sincerest thanks are also due to all the other people for their invaluable help in compiling this Volume.

Also I feel equally indebted to BPB publication which has given me opportunity to collaborate and taken responsibility to publish my books.

Interview Questions Series

.Net Interview Questions

By: Shivprasad Koirala

ISBN: 9788183331470

₹330/-

Networking Interview Questions

By: Shivprasad Koirala
Shaam Sheikh

ISBN: 97881836332439

₹270/-

Software Testing Interview Questions

By: Shivprasad Koirala

ISBN: 9788183332361

₹297/-

Project Management Interview Questions

By: Shivprasad Koirala
Shaam Sheikh

ISBN: 9788183332576

₹297/-

SQL Server Interview Questions

By: Shivprasad Koirala

ISBN: 9788183331036

₹297/-

Jave/J2EE Interview Questions

By: Shivprasad Koirala

ISBN: 9788183331739

₹297/-

SharePoint Interview Questions & Answers

By: Shivprasad Koirala

ISBN: 978818333092

₹240/-

Interview Questions In C Programming

By: Yashavant Kanethkar

ISBN: 9788183332934

₹399/-

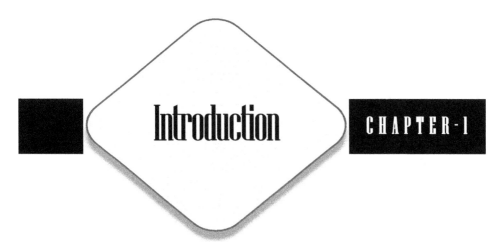

Introduction

CHAPTER-1

What is AutoCAD?

Autodesk Company who develop a software named AutoCAD, stands for Autodesk's computer aided design.

It's a drafting and designing software, whether there are several software for drafting and designing are available in market, Out of them The AutoCAD is best, because it works on co-ordinate system, that help's in survey drawing and drafting.

History of AutoCAD?

AutoCAD was Came in concept during 1977, and it's first commercial release was in 1979 with the name Interact CAD. Later on Autodesk Company develop it and release in 1982 for Microcomputer. Gradually the lighter version for small PC and notebook were release.

In 2010 AutoCAD 360 app was released for mobile.

Usage of AutoCAD

AutoCAD is used for 2D and 3D design, mostly for Civil, Mechanical & Architecture domain. You can design & draw layout, building plan, mechanical part etc.

This software is very popular among small to large scale Companies.

What is New in AutoCAD 2017?

Every year AutoCAD new version is released with some new tools and feature as well as carrying previous feature.

AutoCAD 2017 is also released with some new feature.

For ex.

Enhanced pdf option used to convert drawing file into pdf.

Dimension tools is also updated in 2017 release.

What is Workspace?

Workspace provides us a platform for carrying out our work with definite sets of menus, toolbars, palettes, which are displayed according to the work space selected. A workspace may also display the ribbon toolbar; it is a distinct palette with task-specific control panels.

One can easily switch between workspaces. We are aided with the following task-based workspaces in AutoCAD 2017:

- 2D Drafting & Annotation
- 3D Modeling
- 3D Basic

Say for example, if we have to create 3D models, we can use the 3D modeling workspace, which provides us only 3D-related toolbars, menus, and palettes. And hides the other interface items that we do not need for 3D modeling, thus maximizing the screen area available for our work.

Depending upon our drawing requirement, we can modify a selected workspace with our choices of tools and pallets and save it as a new workspace with a different name for easy access in future use.

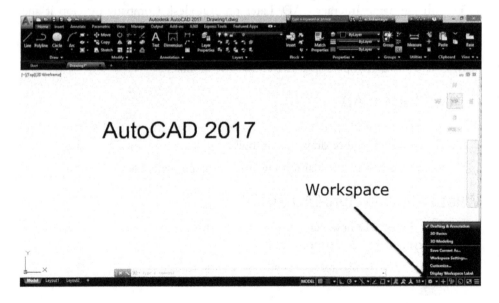

Overview

CHAPTER-2

Welcome Screen

It is the first time that Autodesk AutoCAD has introduced a welcome screen in its version of 2017. In this version when we open the AutoCAD we get to see a welcome screen. The welcome screen provides easy learning, starting, and exploring AutoCAD. In this screen, we will get to see two different types of tab at the bottom namely LEARN and CREATE. In this version, we can add the number of new tab according to our requirement. When we choose to add a new tab, we get Create page by default.

■ What is NEW TAB CREATE?

In this tab, we will have three columns providing us options to proceed as per our requirement.

Three columns namely Get Started, Recent Documents and Get connected. The name of columns gives us a notion of its use. Let's begin with "GET STARTED" it is for starting a fresh new drawing page, or we can work upon our previously drawn file by browsing the folder. Next is "RECENT DOCUMENT" this column

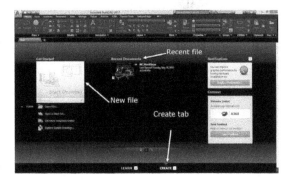

provides instant access to the file that we lastly worked upon in AutoCAD. And finally "GET CONNECTED" provides us web access to Autodesk 360 and also shows us notifications (if any) regarding AutoCAD.

■ What is NEW TAB LEARN?

Day by day increasing use of AutoCAD is attracting new users, Keeping this in mind AutoCAD 2017 comes with a learn tab providing its new users easy learning via its three columns namely: What's new, Getting Started Videos and TIP/Online Resources.

GUI Overview

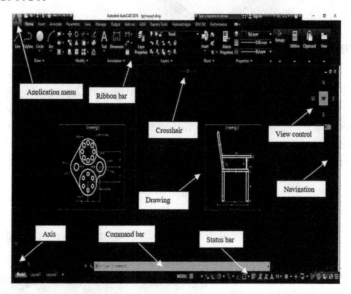

Mouse use

Left button of mouse is used to CLICK and Right button is used for ENTER.

To move the AutoCAD page press the scroll button and move the mouse. If u have to do zoom in and zoom out the page just revolve the scroll button.

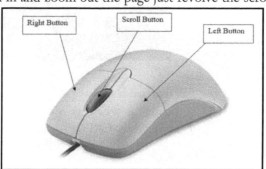

Difference between Command Work & Visual Work

AutoCAD provide two mode of operation, first is Command based work and another is visual work.

When you work using GUI (Graphical User Interface) for ex. using tools icon this is visual work and

When you do same thing using command that is command work.

For Ex. if u have to draw line using command write L in command bar and press ENTER,

And if u want to draw using visual click on line Icon.

Coordinate System with Line Command

Our AutoCAD page is based on graphical coordinate system that constitutes three axis viz. x, y, z. As we know these three axis starts from a point origin (0, 0, 0) one in the vertical direction, next horizontal and the last parallel to the page. Moving forward in any of the axes increases the value of the coordinate in that axis.

We can draw using any of the three coordinates system given below:

■ Absolute Coordinate System (X, Y)

We use absolute coordinate system when we know the precise distance of x coordinate and y coordinate from the origin.

Command: L ↵

Step 1: Specify first point: 0, 0 ↵

Step 2: Specify next point or [Undo]: 8, 0 ↵

Step 3: Specify next point or [Undo]: 8, 2 ↵

Step 4: Specify next point or [Close/Undo]: 6, 2 ↵

Step 5: Specify next point or [Close/Undo]: 6, 4 ↵

Step 6: Specify next point or [Close/Undo]: 2, 4 ↵

Step 7: Specify next point or [Close/Undo]: 0, 2 ↵

Step 8: Specify next point or [Close/Undo]: C ↵

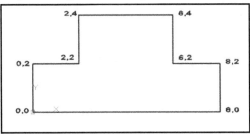

■ Relative Rectangular Coordinate System (@X, Y)

We use this coordinate system when we have a relative distance, i.e., distance of the next point with respect to previous drawn point.

Command: L ↵

Step 1: Specify first point: 2, 2 ↵

Step 2: Specify next point or [Undo]: @3, 0 ↵

Step 3: Specify next point or [Undo]: @0, 1 ↵

Step 4: Specify next point or [Close/Undo]: @-1, 0 ↵

Step 5: Specify next point or [Close/Undo]: @0, 1 ↵

Step 6: Specify next point or [Close/Undo]: @-1, 0 ↵

Step 7: Specify next point or [Close/Undo]: @0, 1 ↵

Step 8: Specify next point or [Close/Undo]: @-1, 0 ↵

Step 9: Specify next point or [Close/Undo]: C ↵

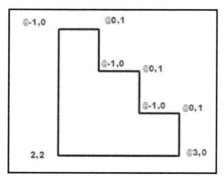

■ Relative Polar Coordinate System (@ distance < angle)

We use relative polar coordinate system when we have a relative distance and angle of a point to draw with respect to the previous point. The use of angle is compulsory in this coordinate system which is measured in Anti clock direction, taking 00 towards the right.

Command: L

Step 1: Specify first point: 2, 3 ↵

Step 2: Specify next point or [Undo]: @100<0 ↵

Step 3: Specify next point or [Undo]: @25<120 ↵

Step 4: Specify next point or [Close/Undo]: @25<90 ↵

Step 5: Specify next point or [Close/Undo]: @15<180 ↵

Step 6: Specify next point or [Close/Undo]: @25<270 ↵

Step 7: Specify next point or [Close/Undo]: @45<180 ↵

Step 8: Specify next point or [Close/Undo]: @25<90 ↵

Step 9: Specify next point or [Close/Undo]: @15<180 ↵

Step 10: Specify next point or [Close/Undo]: @25<270 ↵

Step 11: Specify next point or [Close/Undo]: C ↵

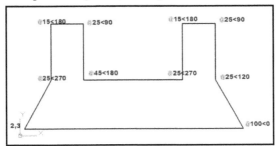

Zoom and Extents

Use the mouse scroll to ZOOM IN ZOOM OUT the drawing created on AutoCAD page, in case scroll does not support then type z in command bar and press enter to zoom.

If created drawing have unexpected size then zoom it and extend after.

Regen

Usually and mostly during zoom in and zoom out of AutoCAD pages, it's not properly work, Or when you move the page it refrain to move, Or when you create circle and wand to view by zoom in it appear like polygon so to resolve these problem use the REGAN command to overcome such type of problem.

When Do We Use Units?

When we begin our new work we start by setting up the units of measurement in which we need to work. When we give the command for unit, we see the Drawing Units dialogue box. The dialogue box is divided into four main sections, namely 'Length,' 'Angle,' 'Insertion Scale.' In "Length" we select our linear units whereas in "Angles," we select our angular units. We can make amendments for linear units and angular units independently and in both sections we can also control the type and precision required. In the Angle section we can also specify the direction of angle as per our requirement and ease.

■ Linear Units

The default unit for length is "Decimal." The AutoCAD 2017 provides five different linear unit types in its box. Brief necessary description of the different units is provided in the table below.

Unit Type	1.5 Drawing Units	1500 Drawing Units	Description
Decimal	1.5000	1500.0000	Metric or SI units
Scientific	1.5000E+00	1.5000E+03	Decimal value raised to a power
Engineering	0'-1.5000"	125'-0.0000"	Feet and decimal inches
Architectural	0'-1 1/2"	125'-0"	Feet and fractional inches
Fractional	1 ½	1500	Whole numbers and fractions

■ Angular Units

As linear, the default angular unit is also decimal and in general circumstances it is not required to be changed. We will find five different angular units provided to us in the units dialogue box. Below is a table describing the necessary description of the types of angular units?

Unit Type	12.5 Angular Units	180 Angular Units	Description
Decimal Degrees	12.500	180.000	Metric units
Deg/Min/Sec	12d30'0"	180d0'0"	Degrees, Minutes and Seconds
Grads	13.889g	200.000g	400 grads = 360 degrees
Radians	0.218r	3.142r	2 Pi radians = 360 degrees
Surveyor	N 77d30'0" E	W	Compass bearings

Step 1: UN Enter in Command bar

Step 2: Click length type

Step 3: Select Architecture

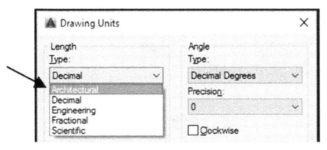

Step 4: Select Feet

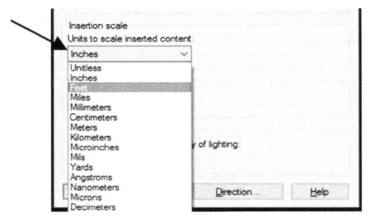

Step 5: Click OK

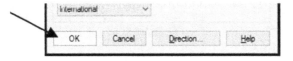

What do you mean by RECTANGLE?

It is a command by which we can make a rectangle having similar right angles and two sides are also similar.

Step 1:- Rec Enter.

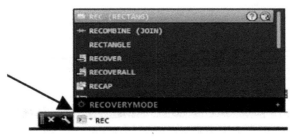

Step 2: Click First point

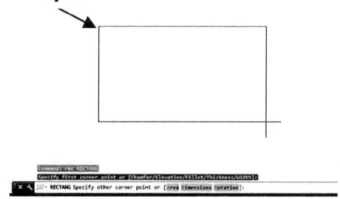

Step 3: Press D Then Enter

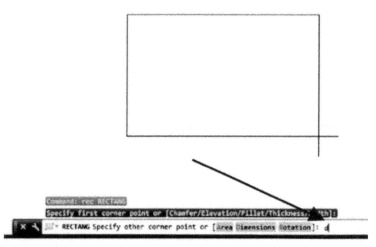

Step 4: length 3' Enter

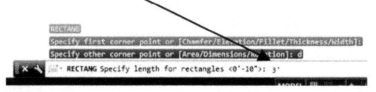

Step 5: width 7' Enter

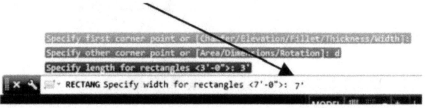

Step 6:- Click other corner point.

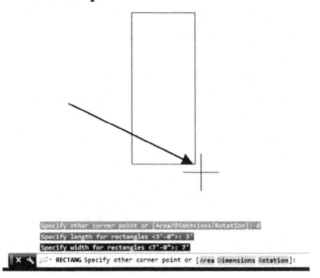

What do you mean by OFFSET?

By using the command offset, we can create a new line, polyline, and arc or circle parallel to the object and at a specified distance from it.

Step 1: O Enter

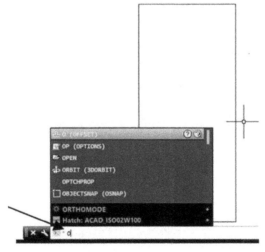

Step 2: Offset distance 5" Enter

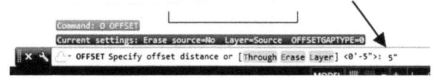

Step 3: Select object

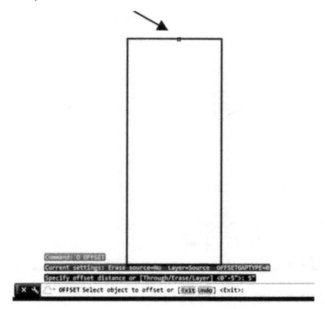

Step 4: Click in Side

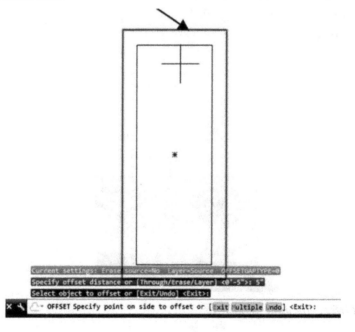

What do you mean by OSNAP?

"OSNAP" means object snap. The Object Snaps are drawing tool that help us in drawing accurately. Osnap specifies us to snap onto a particular point location while picking a point. For example, using Osnap we can sharply pick the end point of a line or the center of a circle. Osnap in AutoCAD is so essential that we cannot draw faultlessly without them.

Step 1: Click Osnap setting icon

Step 2: Click Select all button

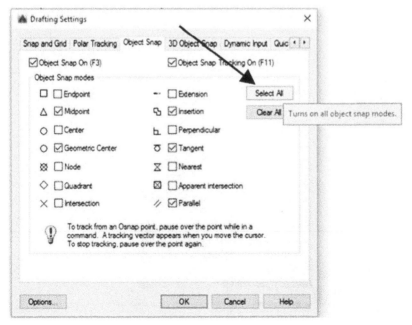

Step 3: Click OK

What do you mean by ARC?

It is a command by which we can create a circle segment (part of a circle) or part of the curve. An arc can be a 2-point or 3-point. In case of 3-point Arc, we can specify the angle, endpoint, and start point, combination of centers, chord length, direction values and radius.

Step 1: A Enter

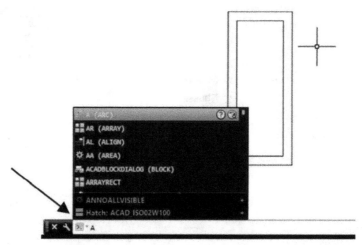

Step 2: C Enter

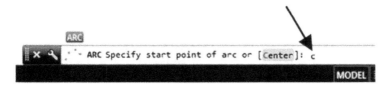

Step 3: Click Midpoint

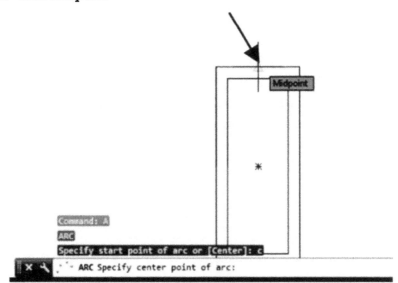

Step 4: Click Start point

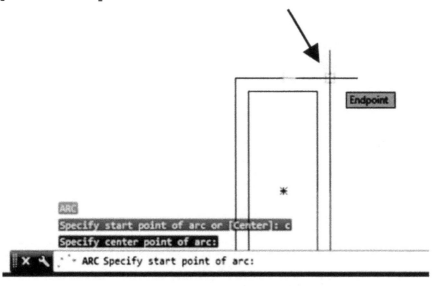

Step 5: Click Endpoint

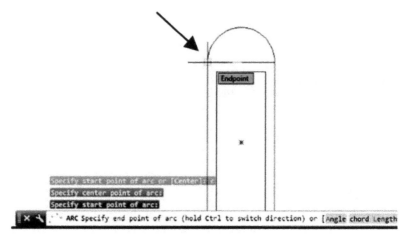

Step 6: A Enter then Click nearest point

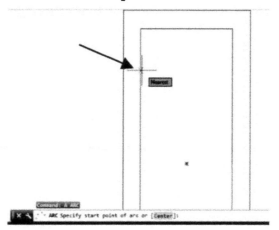

Step 7: Click Second point

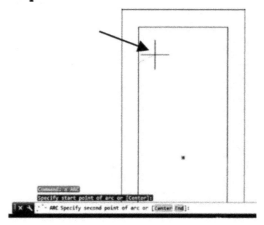

Step 8: Click End point

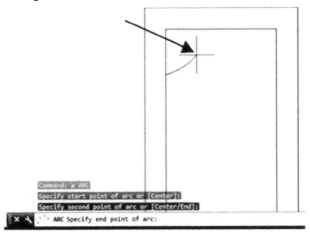

What do you mean by MIRROR?

We use the mirror command to create a reflection of a designated objected about a specified axis.

Step 1:- MI enter then select object.

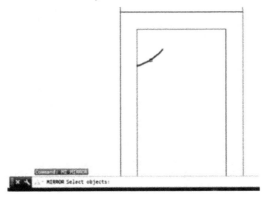

Step 2: Click first point of mirror line

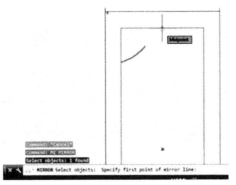

Step 3: Click second point of mirror line

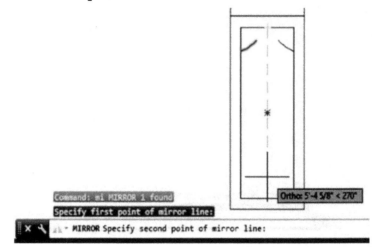

Step 4: N Enter

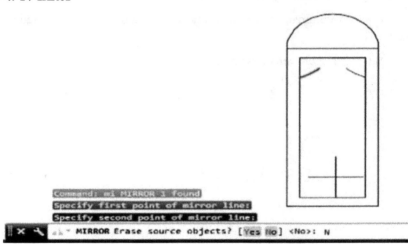

Step 5: A Enter then Create Arc

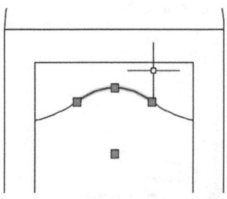

Step 6: MI Enter and select object

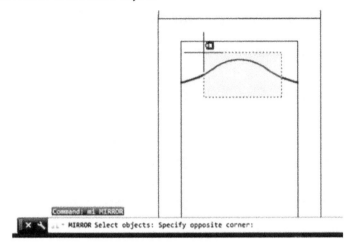

Step 7: Click first point and click second point

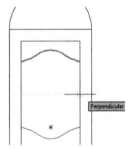

Step 8: N Enter

What do you mean by JOIN?

By using Command join, we can attach two objects lying in the same plane.

Step 1: J Enter

Step 2: Select object then Enter

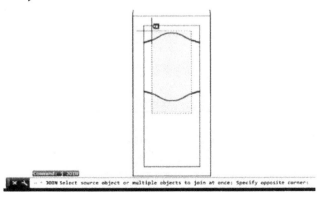

Step 3: O Enter and offset distance 3" Enter

Step 4: Select object and Point on side

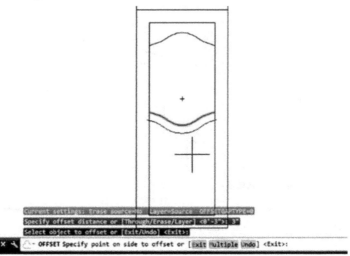

Step 5: L Enter and click first point

Step 6: Click Second point

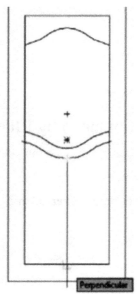

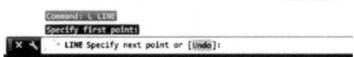

Step 7: O Enter and Offset distance 2" Enter

Step 8: Select object and point on first side

Step 9: Select object and point on second side

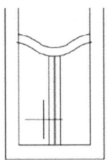

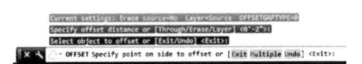

What do you mean by EXTEND?

By using the command extend, we can elongate or say lengthen a line, arc or polyline to meet a specified boundary edge.

Step 1: Press EX and Double Enter

Step 2: Pick on line

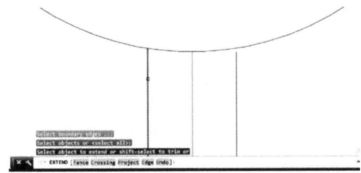

Step 3: Pick on second line

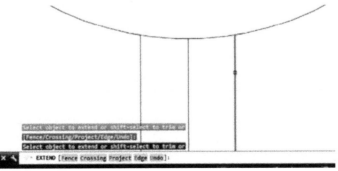

What do you mean by TRIM?

We use command trim to erase a portion of the selected object that crosses a specified edge. In other words, we can use command trim on an object to meet edges of another object.

Step 1: Press TR and double Enter

Step 2: Pick on object

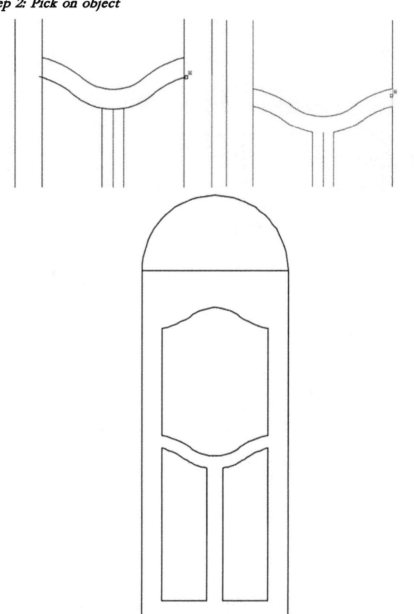

Grill Design

CHAPTER-4

What do you mean by GRID & SNAP?

The grid is a pattern of straight lines that crosses over each other, forming square. In AutoCAD it is infinite in the given workspace. Grid helps us in aligning objects and visualizing the distances between them. Horizontal lines are said to be minor grid lines and vertical lines are said to be major grid lines.

Snap mode limits the movement of the crosshairs since it is defined. With Snap mode on, the cursor will follow an invisible rectangular grid. Snap is helpful in specifying precise points with the arrow keys.

Both are independent to each other but sometimes we use them simultaneously.

Step 1: Click Grid & Snap setting icon

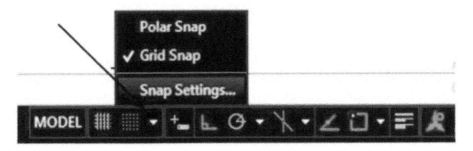

Step 2: Give 5" Grid x spacing

Step 3: Give 5" Grid y spacing

Step 4: Give 5" Snap x spacing

Step 5: Give 5" Snap x spacing

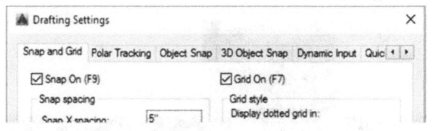

Step 6: Click Snap on

Step 7: Click Grid on

Step 8: Click Ok

What do you mean by PLINE?

Command Pline stands for polyline and is same as line and created in the same way as line is created but it requires 1st and 2nd endpoints. It is an object but may have different segments. In polyline, each segment can be given required width and can be also given different width to the start and end of the polyline.

Step 1: PL Enter and click Start point

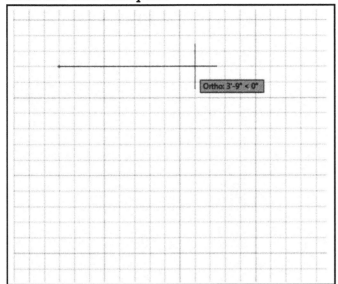

Step 2: Click first point

Step 3: Click second, third......................Twenty point

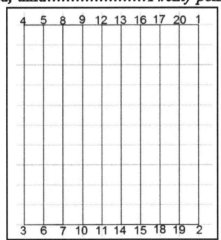

What do you mean by ELLIPSE?

It is a command to create an Elliptical type arc. The first two points determine the location and length of the first axis whereas the third point fixes the distance from the center of the ellipse to the end point of the second axis.

Step 1: EL Enter then C enter for center

Step 2: Click center point

Step 3: Click Endpoint

Step 4: Click Endpoint

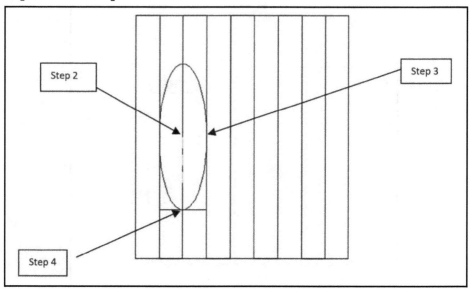

Step 5: Step 1, 2, 3, 4 again repeat

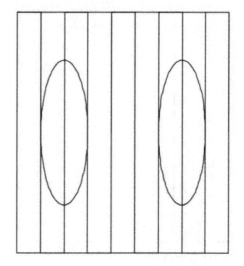

What do you mean by LAYERS?

It is a command having large space where all types of object are placed, and the basic designing is done on it.

On starting AutoCAD default layer is only shown which is set current. The person using it defines other different layers. The object defined is only seen on the layer, layer itself is not seen. Layer is invisible matter…..

Step 1: LA Enter and click new layer

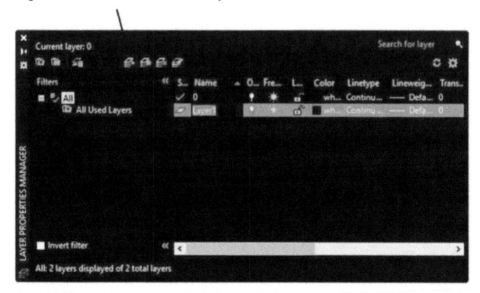

Step 2: Change layer name And Again click new layer

Step 3: Change layer color

Step 4: Change line thickness

Step 5: Tab close

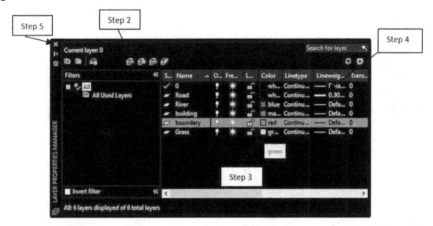

Step 6: Click layer

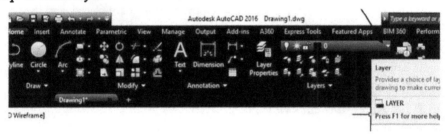

Step 7: Select boundary layer

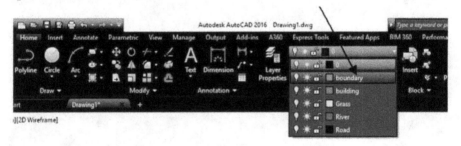

Step 8: REC Enter and create a rectangle

Step 9: Select River layer (Like Step 6-7)

What do you mean by SPLINE?

It is a command making smooth curves and can be constructed along specific points.

Step 1: SPL Enter and click first point

Step 2: Click second, third.......seven point

Step 3: Then enter

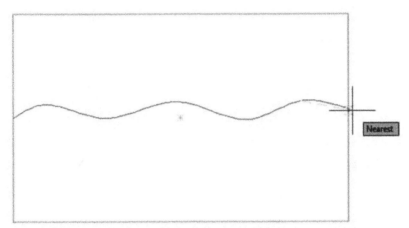

Step 4: O Enter and click on line and second click

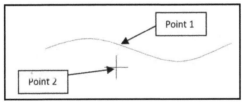

Step 5: Select object and pick on side

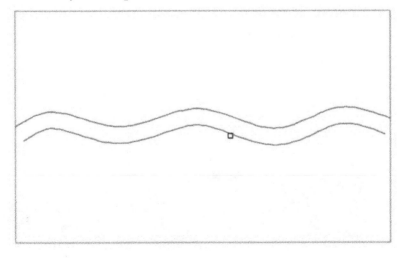

Step 6: L Enter and close spline

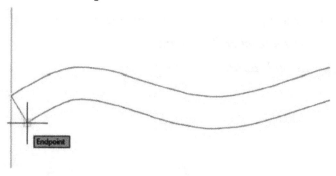

What do you mean by MLINES OR MULTILINES?

It is a command to create multi-parallel straight lines.

Step 1: ML Enter and click start point

Step 2: Click next point and enter

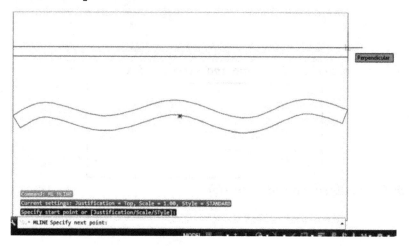

What do you mean by HATCH?

It is a command to create lines for section viewing and filling of an area of an object so that it is distinguished from other objects.

Step 1: H Enter and click pattern

Step 2: Select AR-CONC

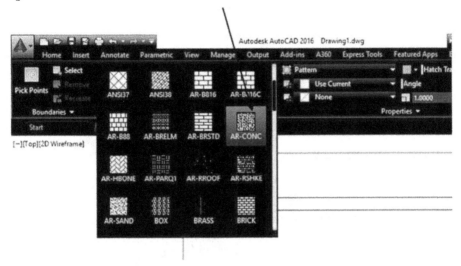

Step 3:- Pick point on road inside

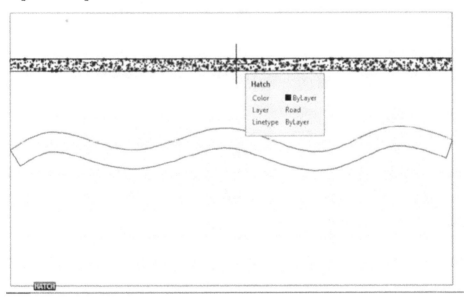

What do you mean by GRADIENT?

Gradient command is used to create a gradient type of fill which means "two color types of filling." This two color types of filling is "transition filling."

Step 1: GD Enter and click pattern

Step 2: Select GR-LINEAR

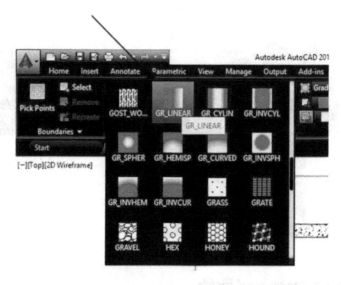

Step 3: Click 2nd color and Turn off color or select White color

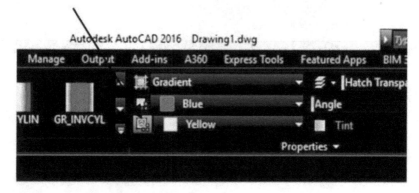

Step 4: Pick point on River inside

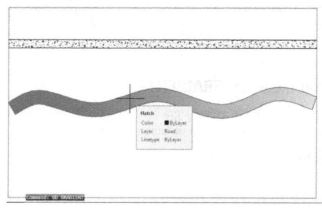

Step 5: H Enter and select grass pattern

Step 6: Then select green color and pick open place (boundary inside)

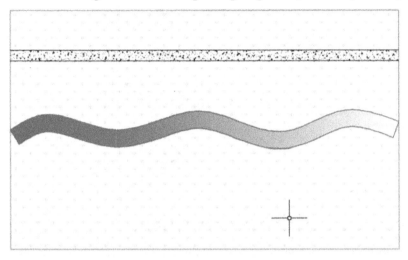

Step 7: PL Enter and create Pline without dimension

What do you mean by MIRROR?

We use the mirror command to create a reflection of a designated objected about a specified axis.

Step 1: MI Enter

Step 2: Select object then Enter

Step 3: Click first point

Step 4: Click second point

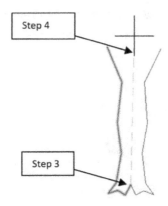

Step 5: N Enter

What do you mean by REVISION CLOUD?

It is a command to highlight the area of the revision cloud. It is a series of arc formed to create a revision cloud.

Step 1: REVCLOUD Enter

Step 2: F Enter for freehand option

Step 3: Click first point

Step 4: Click second point

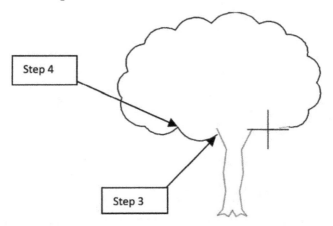

Step 5:- H Enter.

Step 6:- Select Grass pattern.

Step 7:- Select green color.

Step 8:- Change hatching scale.

Step 9:- Pick point.

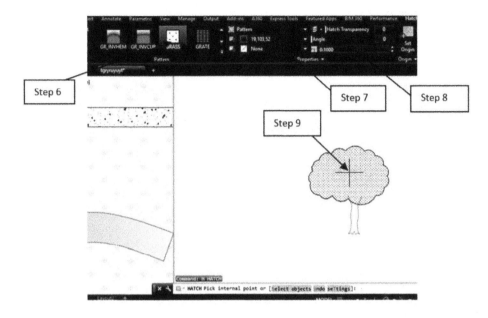

What do you mean by BLOCKS?

It is used to create a block by selecting that object and giving it an insertion point and then save it by the name of itself. These blocks are saved in the design center toolbar and the tool palettes.

Step 1: Select Object then B Enter

Step 2: Give block name

Step 3: Click pick point

Step 4: Click a point

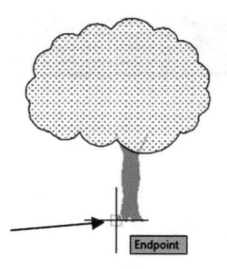

Step 5: Click OK

What do you mean by INSERT?

INSERT is use to insert the pre-created block.

Step 1: I Enter then click OK

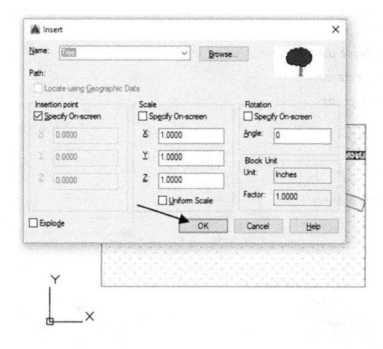

Step 2: Click on drawing

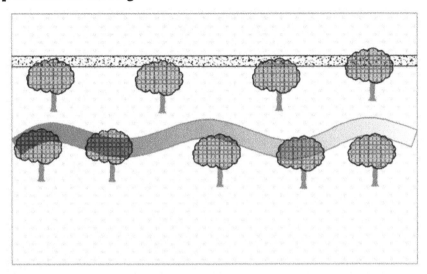

What do you mean by TEXT?

It is a command to create a single-line text object. It is sometimes used to define different line text objects which we can modify, relocate.

Step 1: DT Enter then click on drawing

Step 2: Enter height

Step 3: Enter rotation angle

Step 4: Enter Text. Like- Ganga River

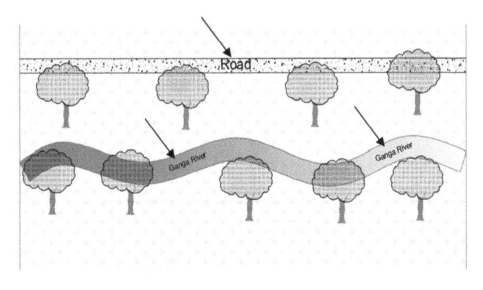

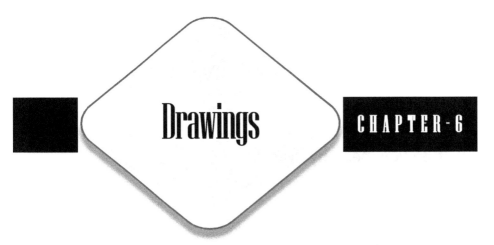

DRAWING 1

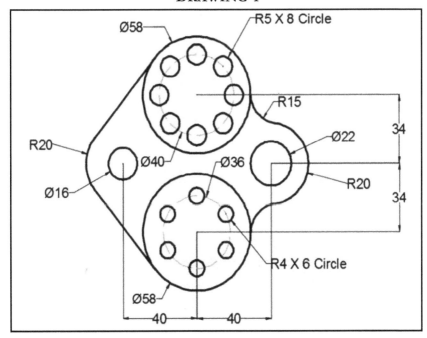

What do you mean by CIRCLE?

It is a command by which we can make a curved line joined in the end having equal distance from the center point. Circle help us to create two-way normal. But in AutoCAD there are three ways to create Circle. One is by specifying the radius and second by specifying Diameter. Besides this 2point, 3point, and tan tan radius. Here we have five ways to create Circle.

Step 1: C Enter then click center point

Step 2: D Enter for diameter then 58 Enter

What do you mean by COPY?

When we need the same object at more than one place, we draw an object once and then use the command 'copy' to use the same object at other places.

Step 1: Select object (circle) then CO Enter

Step 2: Click center point for base point

Step 3: Specify direction for second point

Step 4: 68 Enter

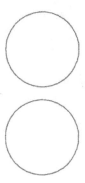

Step 5: C Enter then Click center point

Step 6: D Enter for diameter then 40 Enter

Step 7: C Enter the Click Second circle center point

Step 8: D Enter for diameter then 36 Enter

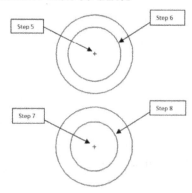

Step 9: Select object then CO Enter

Step 10: Click center point for base point

Step 11: Specify direction for second point

Step 12: 34 Enter for distance

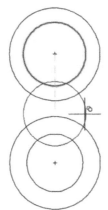

What do you mean by MOVE?

By using move we select an object, then select its base point and move it to the required position and direction.

Step 1: Select object then M Enter

Step 2: Click center point for base point

Step 3: Specify direction for second point

Step 4: 40 Enter for distance

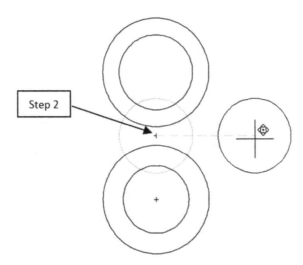

Step 5: C Enter then click center point

Step 6: 11 Enter for radius

Step 7: Select object then CO Enter

Step 8: Click center point for base point

Step 9: Specify direction for second point

Step 10: 80 Enter for distance

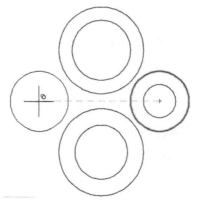

Step 11: C Enter then click center point

Step 12: 8 Enter for radius

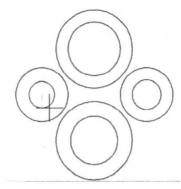

Step 13: C Enter then click center point

Step 14: 5 Enter for radius

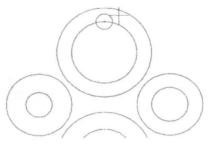

Step 15: C Enter then click center point

Step 16: 4 Enter for radius

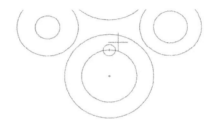

What do you mean by ARRAY?

We use command array for creating a series of object in a continuous manner and the required number over rectangular, polar (circular) or any selected path.

■ They are Three Types

Rectangular

Rectangular Array can be copied to multiple objects. Rectangular Array object is a copy of the row and column where we can give the distance between rows and columns.

Path

Polar Array of objects in multiple copies can be made in a circular pattern. Array Polor by the center point and the number and angle of the object copy is given to the use of Polor Array. Copy of which may be circular object.

Polar

Array path, the path of an object like any other object copies. The second object path which does work. The Curve is the path.

Step 1: Select object then AR Enter

Step 2: PO Enter for Array type

Step 3: Click center point for center base point

Step 4: 8 items Enter for 8 circle

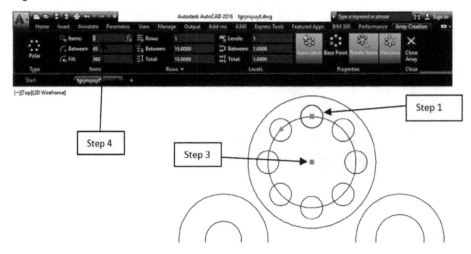

Step 5: Select object then AR Enter

Step 6: PO Enter for Array type

Step 7: Click center point

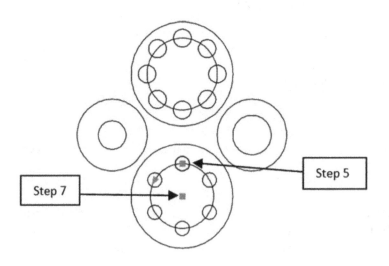

Step 8: C Enter

Step 9: T Enter for Tangent circle

Step 10: Click first tangent point

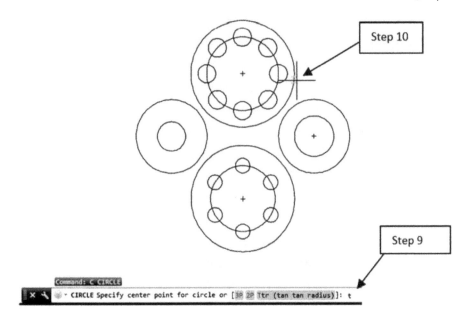

Step 11: Click second tangent point

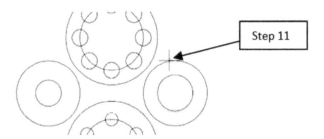

Step 12: 15 Enter for tangent radius

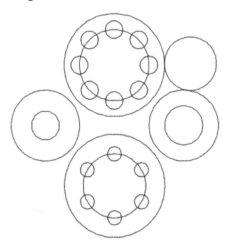

Step 13: TR double Enter

Step 14: Click object

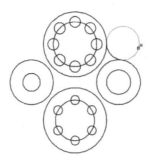

Step 15: Select object then MI Enter

Step 16: Click first point for mirror axis

Step 17: Click second point for mirror axis

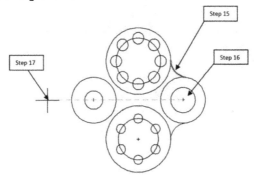

Step 18: N Enter for erase no source object

Step 19: Click OSNAP Setting

Step 20: Click clear all then select only tangent

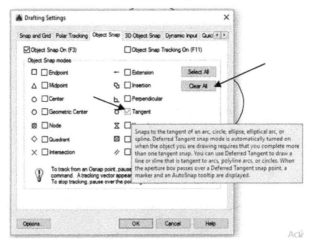

Step 21: Click OK

Step 22: L Enter then click first tangent point

Step 23: Click second tangent point

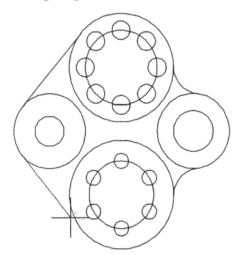

Step 24: TR double Enter

Step 25: Click object

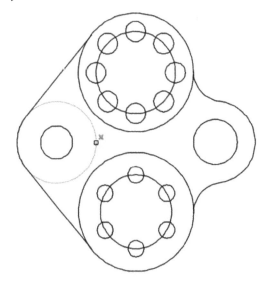

DRAWING 2

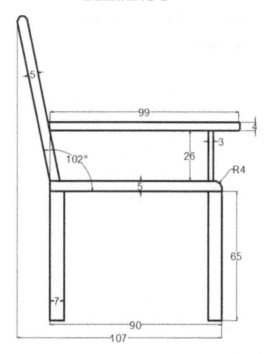

Step 1: REC Enter then click first corner point

Step 2: D Enter for dimension

Step 3: 90 Enter for Length

Step 4: 5 Enter for width

Step 5: Click opposite corner

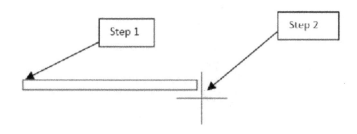

Step 6: L Enter then click first point

Step 7: Specify direction and 65 Enter

Step 8: Specify direction and 7 Enter

Step 9: Specify direction and 65 Enter

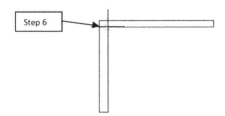

Step 10: Select object then MI Enter

Step 11: Click first point for mirror axis

Step 12: Click second point

Step 13: N Enter For no

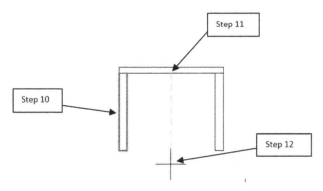

What do you mean by EXPLODE?

Command Explode breaks a block, hatch pattern or dimension into its constituent entities and polyline into a series of straight lines. By using explode, we can also modify the properties of a particular object in block, etc.

Step 1: Select object then X Enter

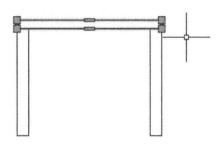

Step 2:O Enter

Step 3: 26 Enter for distance

Step 4: Select object then click on side

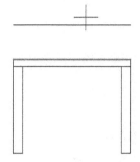

Step 5: O Enter

Step 6: 4 Enter for distance

Step 7: Select object then click on side

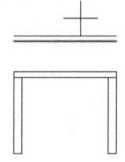

Step 8: L Enter then click first point

Step 9: Click second point then enter

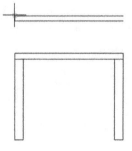

Step 10: O Enter

Step 11: 99 Enter for distance

Step 12: Select object then click on side

What do you mean by EXTEND?

By using the command extend, we can elongate or say lengthen a line, arc or polyline to meet a specified boundary edge.

Step 1: EX double Enter

Step 2: Click on first object

Step 3: Click on Second object

Step 4: L Enter then click first point

Step 5: Specify direction and 107 Enter

Step 6: Specify direction and click without dimension

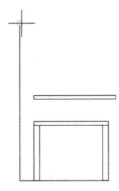

Step 7: L Enter then click first point

Step 8: Click second point then Enter

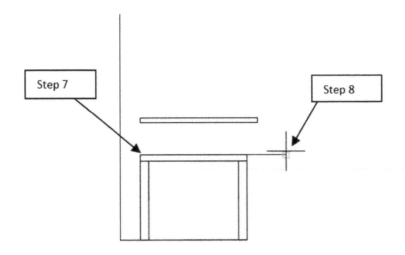

What do you mean by ROTATE?

By using the command rotate, we can give inclination to an object from an axis.

Step 1: Select object then RO Enter

Step 2: Click base point

Step 3: 102 Enter for angle

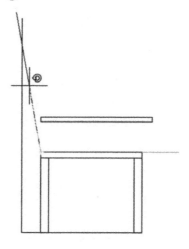

Step 4: TR double Enter

Step 5: Click on object

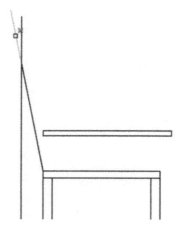

What do you mean by ERASE?

As the word suggests, we use erase to remove an unwanted object from our drawing.

Step 1:- Select object then E Enter.

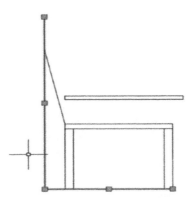

Step 2: O Enter

Step 3: 5 Enter for distance

Step 4: Click on side

Step 5: EX double Enter

Step 6: Click on object

Step 7: L Enter then click first point

Step 8: Click second point then Enter

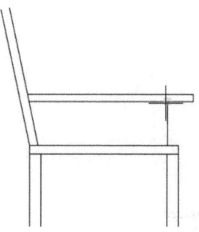

Step 9: O Enter

Step 10: 3 Enter for distance

Step 11: Select object then click on side

What do you mean by FILLET?

We use the command fillet when need to construct an arc of specified radius between two lines, arcs, circles or vertices of polylines.

Step 1: F Enter

Step 2: R Enter for radius

Step 3: 4 Enter then select first object

Step 4: Select second object

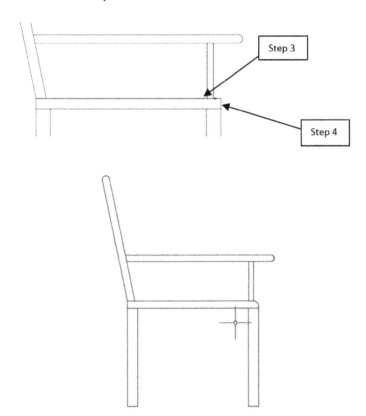

What do you mean by ALIGN?

We use command Align when we need to keep an object in scale with another object i.e. it used for aligning one or more point of an object called source point with the points of other object called definition point.

Step 1: Select object then AL Enter

Step 2: Click first Source point

Step 3: Click first destination point

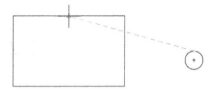

Step 4: Click second source point

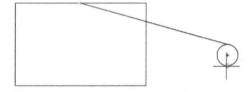

Step 5: Click second destination point

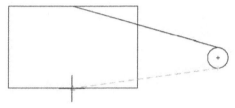

Step 6: Enter for continue

Step 7: Y Enter for scale objects based

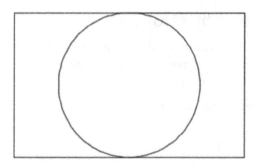

What do you mean by BREAK?

By using command break, we can erase part of the line, arc or a circle or used to split it into two lines or arc. Generally, we use it for creating a gap between lines for writing text.

Step 1: BR Enter then select object

Step 2: F Enter for first point

Step 3: Click first point

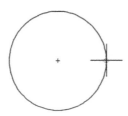

Step 4: Click second point

What do you mean by CHAMFER?

A chamfer is an angled line connection, by using command chamfer we create an angled connection at the intersection of two lines.

Step 1: CHA Enter

Step 2: D Enter for distance

Step 3: 20 Enter for first chamfer distance

Step 4: 10 Enter for second chamfer distance

Step 5: Select first object

Step 6: Select second object

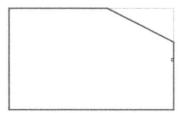

What do we mean by DIVIDE?

When we use the command divide, it places a point along the line, arc, circle, polyline dividing it into the required number of segments.

Step 1: DIV Enter then select object

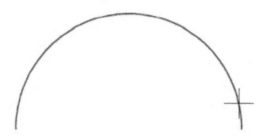

Step 2: 10 Enter for number of segments

Step 3: PDMODE Enter for point style

Step 4: 3 Enter for cross type

When do we use MEASURE?

When we need to place points at specific required intervals along the line, polyline, arc or circle we use the command measure.

Step 1: ME Enter then select object

Step 2: 3 Enter for length of segments

What do you mean by SCALE?

By using command scale, we can alter the size of an object proportionally.

Step 1: Select object then SC Enter

Step 2: Click base point

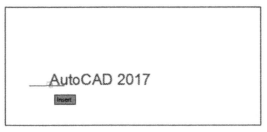

Step 3: R Enter for reference

Step 4: 1 Enter for reference length

Step 5: 2 Enter for new length

AutoCAD 2017

What do you mean by POLYGON?

It is a command by which we can create a plane figure having at least three straight sides and angles. Triangle, rectangle and pentagon can be created through this command. In AutoCAD we can construct a polygon object that has a minimum of three closed sides and maximum of 1024 sides. There are two type Polygon. First inscribed in the circle and second circumscribed about circle.

■ Inscribed in the Circle

In this the polygon lies inside the circle with its vertices on the circumference.

Step 1: POL Enter

Step 2: 6 Enter for Polygon side (Min 3 Max 1024)

Step 3: Click center point for polygon center

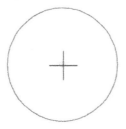

Step 4: I Enter for inscribed in circle

Step 5: 10 Enter for radius

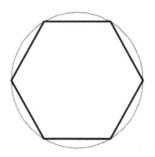

■ Circumscribed about Circle

It is a polygon constructed such that circles lies within it and its circumference crosses through the mid-points of the vertices of polygon.

Step 1: POL Enter

Step 2: 6 Enter for Polygon side (Min 3 Max 1024)

Step 3: Click center point for polygon center

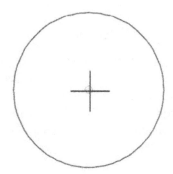

Step 4:- C Enter for circumscribed about circle.

Step 5:- 10 Enter for radius.

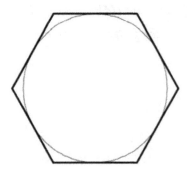

What do you mean by POINT?

We used point to create point objects. With the help of this command we specify the 3d location for a point, can snap objects, view current elevation (if we neglect the z axis.)

Step 1: PO Enter then pick point

Step 2: PDMODE Enter for point style

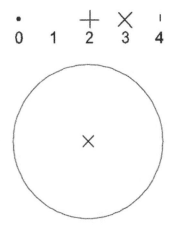

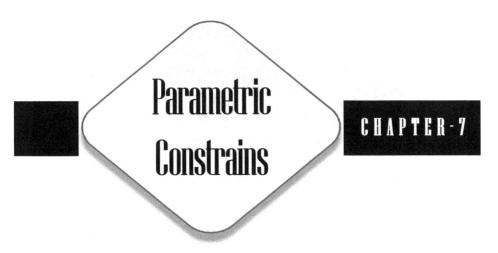

Parametric Drawings

■ What is meant by PARAMETRIC DRAWINGS?

By using Parametric constraints, we can force an object to behave the way we want it to.

If we need an object to behave the same way as other we need to set a constraint on it to do the same.

For example, if we need a pair of line to always remain parallel to one another we can select constraint parallel, then even if we change the position of any one object the other will also change accordingly being always parallel to the first.

In the Parametric tool panels, Constraints are divided into three sections:

1. Geometric Constraints
2. Dimensional Constraints
3. Manage

RIBBON: PARAMETRIC

MENU: PARAMETRIC

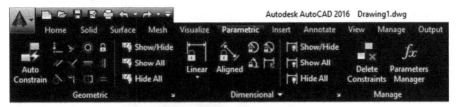

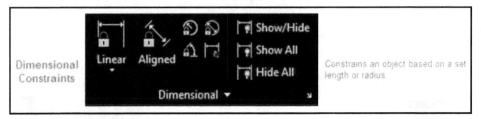

Geometric Constraints

Ribbon: Parametric ⟩ Geometric

Menu: Parametric Constraints

Geometric constraints associate geometric objects together. For example, If we have a symmetric drawing and later we make a change in the drawing, now the work will no longer remain symmetric, to maintain symmetricity of the drawing we apply the constraints symmetry and select the objects that we require to keep symmetrical.

Let's say we have a rectangle. As for rectangle, sides have to be perpendicular to each other. But in case during the design, we may need to change the position of a vertex. If we extend one of the rectangle vertex, then it would not remain a rectangle anymore. As AutoCAD is not aware that we want to keep it as a rectangle.

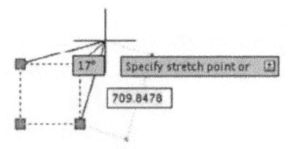

To prevent this, in AutoCAD, we apply perpendicular constraints, ensuring that we want them always perpendicular to each other. So now we add a perpendicular constraint to the two sides. Now, try to stretch the vertex again.

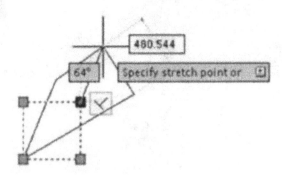

As we can see, the two sides are perpendicular to each other. But the other edges don't. So, We need to add all constraint to keep it a rectangle.

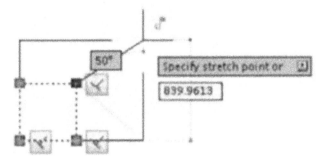

Dimensional Constraints

Dimensional constraints are different to geometrical; these are used in making changes to what we have already worked with. If we have a drawing and we need to make amendments in the dimensions of the objects we use dimensional constraints

Instead of making a line vertical (for example), we can make a line 10 units long and make it stay that way until we change it. We can add more than one dimensional constraint on certain objects.

Draw a random angled line on the screen. Pick on the Aligned constraint icon.

 Pick two points on the line.
Aligned

Notice that even if we have our Osnaps off, we can only pick the endpoints and midpoint on the line. After selecting the 2 points, we can now enter a length that we want the distance between those points to be.

With the constraint still highlighted, enter a number. D3 in this example refers to the 3rd-dimensional constraint in the drawing. If we add a constraint from end to middle, add another from end to end (or vice versa). Notice that the constraint will be double the first one. If we change one, the other will change accordingly.

How To Manage Constraints?

In the third column of parametric toolbar we have 'manage' section. In this section we can perform two operations, we can use "parameters manager" to generate excel sheets of all the constraints used and secondly "delete constraints" to remove unnecessary constraints.

By using Parameter manager, the excel sheet of parameter is generated, using this sheet we can also make changes in the sheet that are simultaneously applied on the objects in the drawing.

Smart Dimension new

Smart Dimension tool is recently introduce in AutoCAD 2017.

This tool is use to show the dimension of an object. This tool has an existing feature which is u can check any dimension of an object. While in normal dimension tool, the dimensions of an object is different like aligned, linear, radius etc. but Smart dimension lonely work on behalf of all dimension.

Step 1: Home ▶ Annotate Dimensions ▶ Dimension

Step 2: Select object

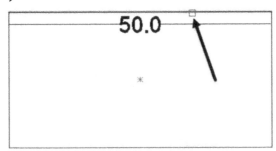

What do you mean by LIST?

When we need to know the all the properties of an object, we use command LIST. It lists all information of the selected objected such as what type of object it is (whether it is a circle, arc, block etc.), what is its color, its axis, its thickness, location of its end points, elevation from z-axis.

Following information we can get through command LIST:

- Line weight, Color, line type.
- How thick the object is..?.
- Z Coordinate elevation.
- Extrusion direction (UCS coordinates), with different Z (0, 0, 1) axis.
- Information related to a particular object type such as for dimensional constraint objects, name, and value; LIST displays the constraint type, reference type (yes or no), expression.

Step 1: Select object then LI Enter

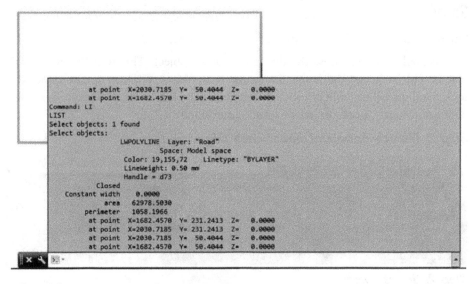

What do you mean by ANGLE?

We use command ANGLE to know the angle between points, circle, or arc.

Step 1: Ribbon Home tabUtilities panelAngle

Step 2: Select arc, circle, line or <Specify vertex>: Select arc

Angle=130⁰

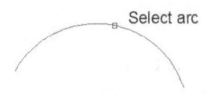

What do you mean by DIST?

DIST is an inquiry command which lists us distance between any two selected points in our command bar.

Step 1: DI Enter then click first point

Step 2: Click second click

And press F2 key

What do you mean by VOLUME?

We use volume command, to compute volume of a defined object.

Step 1: Ribbon Home tabUtilities panelVolume

Step 2: Click first point

Step 3: Click second point

Step 4: Click third point

Step 5: Click forth point

Step 6: T Enter for total

Step 7: 5 Enter for height

Volume=1250.00

What do you mean by AREA?

We use the command area to calculate the area of an object or shape. Using this command, we can calculate the area of the object such as circle or by selecting the various points of a given object etc.

Step 1: AA Enter

Step 2: Click first point

Step 3: Click second point

Step 4: Click third point

Step 5: Click forth point

Step 6: T Enter for total

And press F2 key

```
AutoCAD Text Window - Drawing1.dwg
Edit
Specify next point or [Arc/Length/Undo/Total] <Total>: t

Area = 250.0000, Perimeter = 70.0000
Command: Specify opposite corner or [Fence/WPolygon/CPolygon]:
Command: AREA

Specify first corner point or [Object/Add area/Subtract area] <Object>: *Canc

Command: Specify opposite corner or [Fence/WPolygon/CPolygon]:
Command: *Cancel*

Command: aa AREA
Specify first corner point or [Object/Add area/Subtract area] <Object>:
Specify next point or [Arc/Length/Undo]:
Specify next point or [Arc/Length/Undo]:
Specify next point or [Arc/Length/Undo/Total] <Total>:
Specify next point or [Arc/Length/Undo/Total] <Total>: t

Area = 250.0000, Perimeter = 70.0000

Command:
```

What do you mean by RADIUS?

As we all know, radius is the distance between the center point and the point on the circle or the half of the diameter. It is a command to measure the radius of a selected circle or arc and display the dimension text having a radius symbol in front of it.

Step 1: Ribbon AnnotateDimensionsRadius

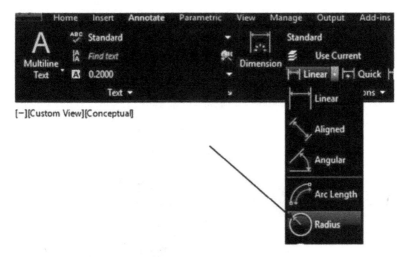

Step 2: Select object

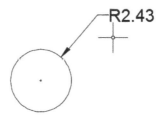

What do you mean by LINEAR?

We use linear command, to create a linear dimension with a vertical, horizontal, or rotated dimension line.

Step 1: Ribbon Annotate tabDimensions panelLinear

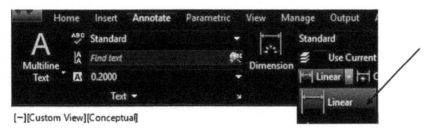

Step 2: Click First point and second point

Step 3: Specify direction and click

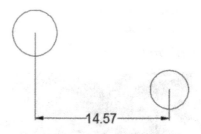

What do you mean by ALIGNED?

It is a command to create a linear dimension in aligned position.

Step 1: Ribbon Annotate tabDimensions panelAligned

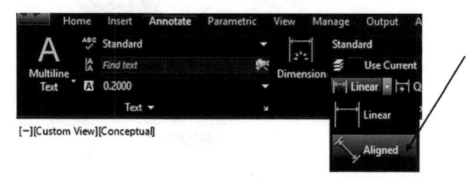

Step 2: Click First point and second point

Step 3: Specify direction and click

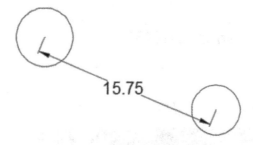

What do you mean by DIAMETER?

It is a command to measure the diameter of the selected circle or arc, display the dimension text with diameter symbol in front of it and can relocate the resulting diameter dimension.

Step 1: Ribbon Annotate tabDimensions panelDiameter

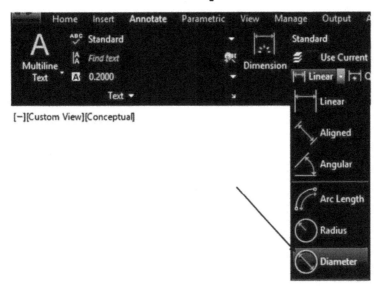

Step 2: Select object

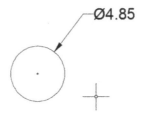

What do you mean by ARC LENGTH?

It is a command to measure the length of a simple arc or polyline arc.

Step 1: Ribbon Annotate tabDimensions panelArc length

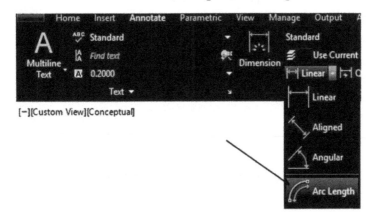

Step 2: Select object

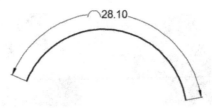

What do you mean by QLEADER?

We use 'QLeader' to create leader annotation. By its help we can set location of set multiline text annotation and specify leader format

You can use QLEADER to:

- Set the location where leaders attach to multiline text annotation
- Specify leader annotation and annotation format
- Constrain the angle of the first and second leader segments.
- Limit the number of leader points

Step 1: LE Enter then click first point

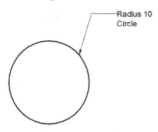

What do you mean by OSNAP ?

"OSNAP" means object snap. The Object Snaps are drawing tool that help us in drawing accurately. Osnap specifies us to snap onto a particular point location while picking a point. For example, using Osnap we can sharply pick the end point of a line or the center of a circle. Osnap in AutoCAD is so essential that we cannot draw faultlessly without them.

Toolbar: Status bar ▶ Osnap

ENDPOINT: The Endpoint command snaps to the end points of arcs, line and to polyline vertices.

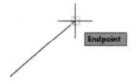

MIDPOINT: The Midpoint command snaps to the mid-point of lines and arcs and to the mid-point of polyline segments.

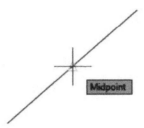

INTERSECTION: The Intersection command snaps to the physical intersection of any two drawing sheet.

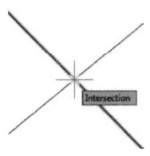

APPARENT INTERSECT: Apparent Intersection command snaps to the point where objects seems to intersect in the current view.

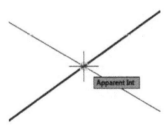

EXTENSION: The Extension command helps to snap to some point along the imaginary extension of the arc, the line, or polyline segment.

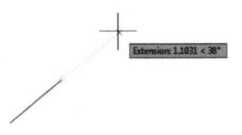

CENTRE: The Centre command snaps to the center of a circle, arc, an object or polyline arc segment.

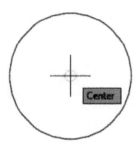

QUADRANT: The Quadrant command locates the four circle quadrant points located at east, north, west and south or 0, 90, 180 and 270 degrees respectively.

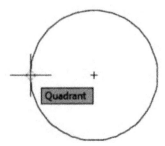

TANGENT: The Tangent command snaps to a tangent point on a circle.

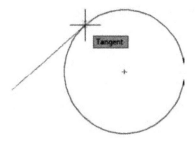

PERPENDICULAR: The Perpendicular command snaps to a point where it forms a perpendicular line with the selected object.

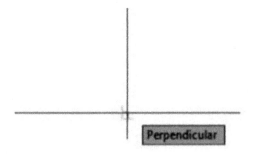

PARALLEL: The parallel command is used to draw a line parallel to a line segment.

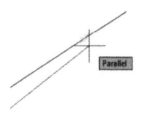

INSERT: The Insert command snaps to the insertion point of the text, block or image.

NODE: The Node command snaps to the center of a Point object.

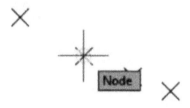

NEAREST: The nearest command snaps the nearest point on the drawing sheet.

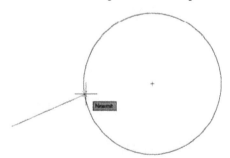

new Geometric Center: Snaps to the Geometric center point of polyline, 2D polyline and 2D spline.

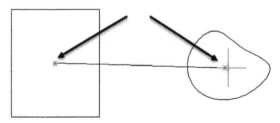

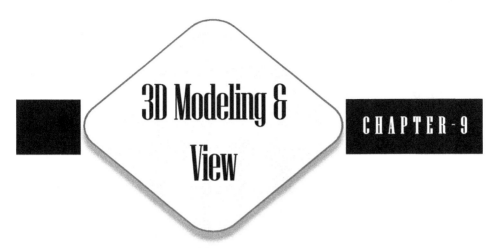

3D Modeling & View

CHAPTER-9

Box

Box is a 3D object. It can be create on X and Y plane and its height create on Z axis. Solid box create by this command.

Step 1: Ribbon ▶ Home tab Modeling Box

Step 2: Click first point for first corner

Step 3: L Enter for box length

Step 4: 60 Enter for length

Step 5: 30 Enter for width

Step 6: 30 Enter for height

Cylinder

Cylinder command is like a circular pipe. To create cylinder we must have radius and height. After creating cylinder on x and y plane give height on z axis.

Step 1: Ribbon ▶ Home tab ▶ Modeling ▶ Cylinder

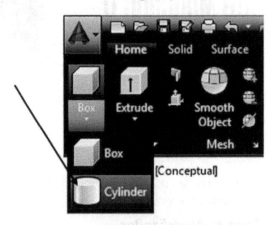

Step 2: Click point for center point

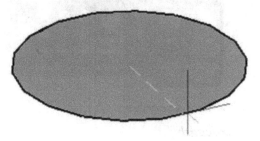

Step 3: 20 Enter for base radius

Step 4: 30 Enter for height

Helix

Helix command creates a spring. Firstly give base radius, top radius and height as well as turns to the use of helix.

Step 1: Ribbon Home tabDrawHelix

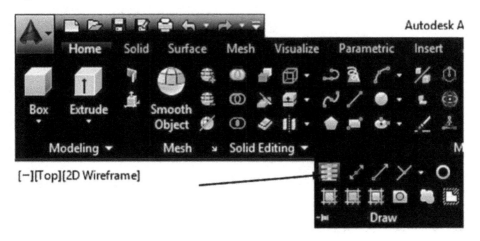

Step 2: Click point for center base point

Step 3:- 20 Enter for base radius.

Step 4:- 30 Enter for top radius.

Step 5:- T Enter for helix turns.

Step 6:- 10 Enter for turns.

Step 7:- 50 Enter for height.

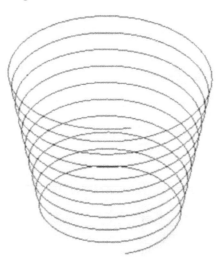

Cone

Cone command is used to create circular cone. To create cone firstly give radius after that give height of cone.

Step 1: Ribbon Home tabModelingCone

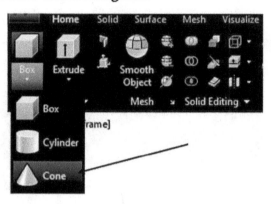

Step 2: Click point for center point

Step 3: 20 Enter for cone radius

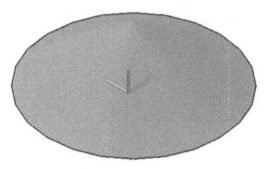

Step 4: 40 Enter for cone height

Torus

Torus command is used to create tube.to create it give radius of circular tube and then give radius her thickness.

Step 1: Ribbon Home tabModelingTorus

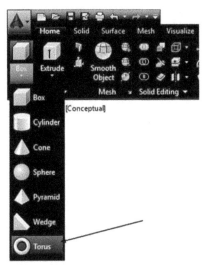

Step 2: Click point for center point

Step 3: 20 Enter for torus radius

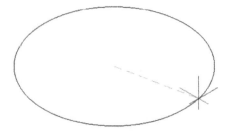

Step 4: 5 Enter for tube radius

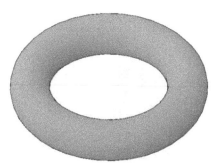

Pyramid

Pyramid command is just like cone, but cone is circular while pyramid have edge, it has at least 3 edge and can up to maximum 32.

Step 1: Ribbon Home tabModelingPyramid

Step 2: Click point for center point

Step 3: 10 Enter for base radius

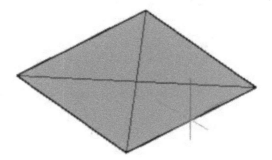

Step 4: 20 Enter for height

Wedge

Sphere command act like a ball, and create just like circle. But circle is 2d object while sphere is a circular shape solid 3d object, and created by giving center and radius.

Step 1: Ribbon Home tabModelingWedge

Step 2: Click first point for wedge corner

Step 3: L Enter for length option

Step 4: 40 Enter for length

Step 5: 20 Enter for width

Step 6: 15 Enter for height

Polysolid

Polysolid command use just like Polyline, but polysolid is a 3d object so we also consider or give thickness and height.

It used to create wall or simple plane (surface).

Step 1: Ribbon Home tabModelingPolysolid

[−][SW Isometric][Conceptual]

Step 2: H Enter for height option

Step 3: 10' Enter for height

Step 4: W Enter for width option

Step 5: 9" Enter for width

Step 6: Click first point

Step 7: Specify direction then 60' Enter

Step 8: Specify direction then 30' Enter

Step 9: Specify direction then 60' Enter

Step 10: C Enter for close

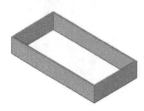

Sphere

Sphere command act like a ball, and create just like circle. But circle is 2d object while sphere is a circular shape solid 3d object, and created by giving center and radius.

Step 1: Ribbon Home tabModelingSphere

Step 2: Click point for center point

Step 3: 20 Enter for radius

Extrude

Extrude command is used to increase the height of object like line, circle, rectangle, arc, spline etc.

That is by increasing height we convert those 2D object into 3D.

For ex. if u take a circle and extend the height u can convert it in to cylinder (3D object) or convert a rectangle into box (I.e. 3D object)

Step 1: Ribbon Home tabModelingExtrude

Step 2: Select 2D object then Enter

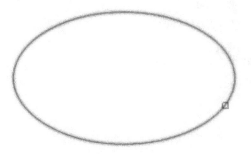

Step 3: 30 Enter for extrude height

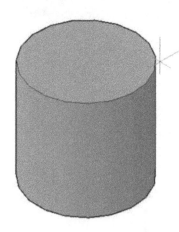

Presspull

Presspull act like extrude command with a significancial difference, it allow to increase or decrease any face of the 3d object while extrude allow only increase height of 2d.

Step 1: Ribbon Home tabModelingPresspull

[−][SW Isometric][Conceptual]

Step 2: Select face for presspull

Step 3: 10 Enter for extrusion height

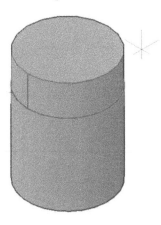

Loft

Loft command is used to convert two or more than two 2d object into single 3d object. Loft command work on any 2d object which is built upon

Any 3rd object by selecting simultaneously both the object and then convert in single 3d object.

To use this command the both object have different Z-axis (i.e. height must be different).

Step 1: Ribbon Home tabModelingLoft

Step 2: Select first object

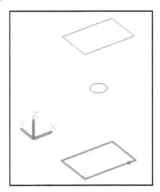

Step 3: Select second object

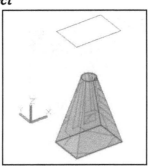

Step 4: Select third object

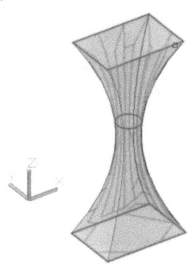

Step 5: Double enter

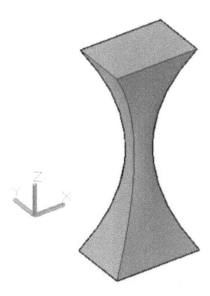

Revolve

Revolve command is use to convert a 2d object into 3d by revolving that object on one of any axis with respect to 2 distinguish point of that axes.

That is chose two different point on that targeted axis and revolve the object circle with respect to that point.

Step 1:- Ribbon Home tabModelingRevolve.

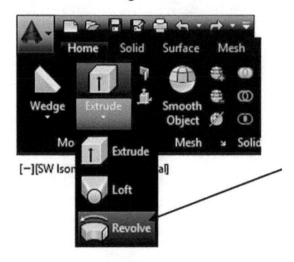

Step 2:- Select 2D object then Enter.

Step 3:- Click first point for Axis.

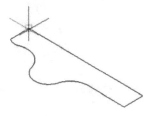

Step 4:- Click second point for Axis.

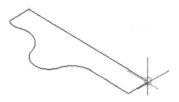

Step 5:- 360 Enter for Circular angle.

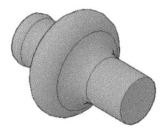

Sweep

Sweep command is used to convert into 3d object by sweeping anyone 2d object to another 2d object.

Step 1: Ribbon Home tabModelingSweep

Step 2: Select object to sweep then Enter

Step 3: Select sweep path

3D Modify Tools

CHAPTER-10

3D move

3d move command is use to move an object along any of the 3 axises. To do that so; select the object first then select 3d move object and u will found all 3 axes appear now move the object along desired axes by click on that axes and provide move distance manually.

Step 1: Ribbon ▶ Home tabModify3D move

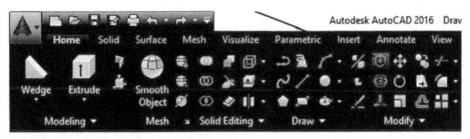

[−][SW Isometric][Conceptual]

Step 2: Select object then Enter

Step 3: Click Z Axis for Z direction move

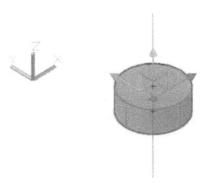

Step 4: 20 Enter for distance

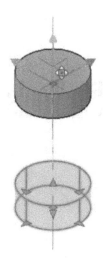

3D rotate

3d rotate command is use to rotate an object along any of the 3 axises. To do that so; select the object first then click on 3d rotate and u see object and u will found all 3 axes appear now rotate the object along desired axes by click on that axes and enter the angle manually as

More u like to rotate from an angle.

Step 1: Ribbon▶Home tab▶Modify▶3D rotate

Step 2: Select object then Enter

Step 3: Click Y axis for about Y axis rotate

Step 4: 90° Enter for rotate angle

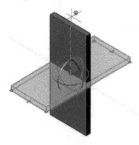

3D scale

3d scale command is used to scale an object along any of three(x or y or z) axis, u can change scale according to length, width or height.

Step 1: Ribbon ▶ Home tab ▶ Modify ▶ 3D scale

Step 2: Select object then Enter

Step 3: Click base point

Step 4: Pick axis

Step 5: R Enter for reference option

Step 6: 1 Enter for reference length

Step 7: 2 Enter for new length

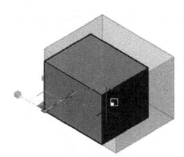

3D Mirror

3d mirror command is used to create reflection or mirror object. But 3d mirror is different than Mirror, we can also mirror an object along z axis.

Step 1: Ribbon ▶ Home tab ▶ Modify ▶ 3D mirror

Step 2: Select object then Enter

Step 3: Click first base point
Step 4: Click second point
Step 5: Click third point

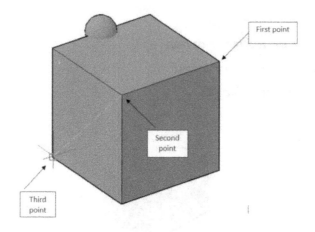

Step 6: N Enter for No, delete source object

3D Array

3d array command is used to create multiple copy of an object simultaneously along all of 3 axis.

Step 1: 3darray Enter

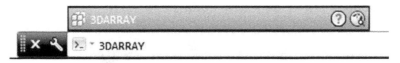

Step 2: Select object then Enter

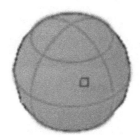

Step 3: R Enter for rectangular option

Step 4: 5 Enter for Rows number

Step 5: 4 Enter for Columns number

Step 6: 3 Enter for Levels number

Step 7: 30 Enter for distance between rows.

Step 8: 30 Enter for distance between columns

Step 9: 30 Enter for distance between levels

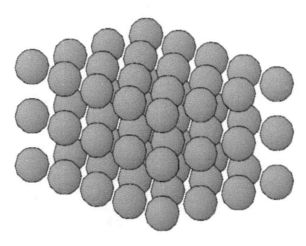

Subtract

Subtract command is used to cut the intersected part of the overlapping 3d object,

For ex if u have to make a circular hole in a box then u have to intersect an object of similar radius then subtract it.

Step 1: Ribbon ▶ Home tab ▶ Solid editing ▶ Subtract

Step 2: Select first object then Enter

Step 3: Select second object

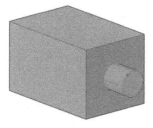

Step 4: Then Enter

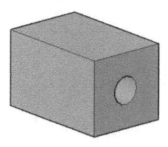

Union

Union command is use to joint or merge two or more than two 3d object.by applying this command all participated object are seems as a block.

Step 1: Ribbon ▶ Home tab ▶ Solid editing ▶ Union

Step 2: Select first object

Step 3: Select second object

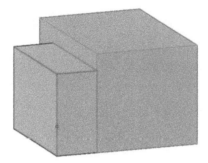

Step 4: Then Enter

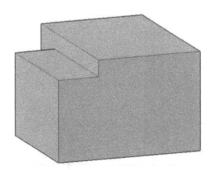

Intersect

Intersect command is use to cut the rest part (i.e. except intersected part) of two 3d object who is intersecting each other.

Step 1: Ribbon ▶ Home tab ▶ Solid editing ▶ Intersect

Step 2: Select first object

Step 3: Select second object

Step 4: Then Enter

Slice

Slice command is use to cut an 3d Object, and remove the isolated part.

Step 1: Ribbon ▶ Home tab ▶ Solid editing ▶ Slice

Step 2: Select object then Enter

Step 3: Pick first point

Step 4: Pick second point

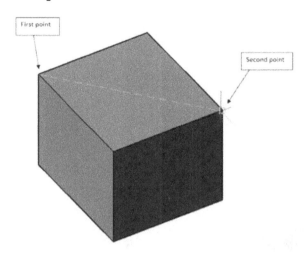

Step 5: Specify a point on desired side

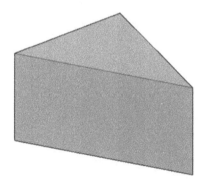

Fillet Edge

Step 1: Ribbon▶Solid▶Solid editing▶Fillet Edge

Step 2:- Select edge then Enter

Step 3:- R Enter for radius option

Step 4:- 3 Enter for fillet radius then Enter

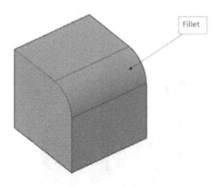

Chamfer Edge

Step 1: Ribbon ▶ Solid ▶ Solid editing ▶ Chamfer Edge

Step 2: Select edge then Enter

Step 3: D Enter for distance option

Step 4: 2 Enter for base distance

Step 5: 2 Enter for other distance then double Enter

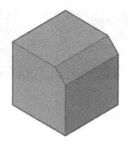

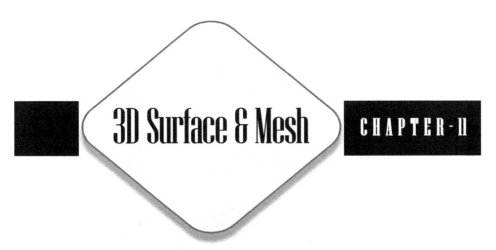

3D Surface & Mesh

CHAPTER-II

Network

A network surface can be created between a network of curves or between the edges of other 3D surfaces or solids.

Step 1: Ribbon ▶ Surface ▶ Create ▶ Network

Step 2: Select all first direction edges then Enter

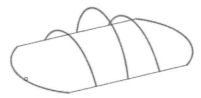

Step 3: Select all second direction edges then Enter

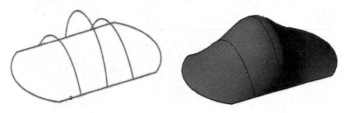

Planar

Create planar surfaces in the space between edge sub objects splines and other 2D and 3D curve.

With PLANESURF, planar surfaces can be created from multiple closed objects and the edges of surface or solid objects. During creation, you can specify the tangency and bulge magnitude.

Step 1: Ribbon ▶ Surface ▶ Create ▶ Planar

Step 2: O Enter for object option

Step 3: Select object then Enter

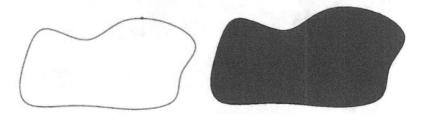

Surface Blend

Creates a continuous blend surface between two existing surfaces.

Step 1: Ribbon ▶ Surface ▶ Create ▶ Blend

Step 2: Select first edge then enter

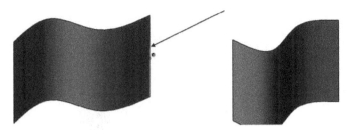

Step 3: Select second edge then enter

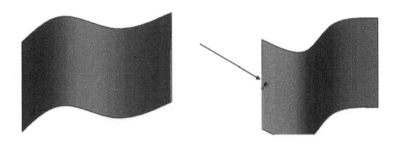

Step 4: Enter

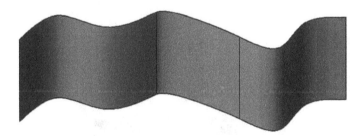

Patch

Creates a new surface by fitting a cap over a surface edge that forms a closed loop.

Step 1: Ribbon ▶ Surface ▶ Create ▶ Patch

Step 2: Select surface edge

Step 3: Double Enter

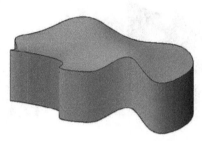

Surface Offset

Create a parallel surface or solid by setting an offset distance from a surface.

Step 1: Ribbon ▶ Surface ▶ Create ▶ Offset

Step 2: Select Object then enter

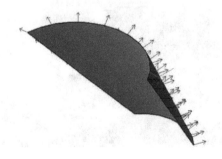

Step 3: 0.1 Enter for offset distance

Surface Extend

Step 1: Ribbon ▶ Surface ▶ Edit ▶ Extend

Step 2: Select surface edge then enter

Step 3 10 Enter for extend distance

Surface Trim

Step 1: Ribbon ▶ Surface ▶ Edit ▶ Trim

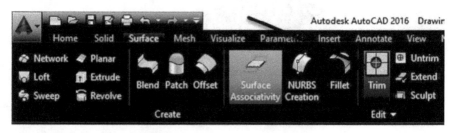

Step 2: Select surface then enter

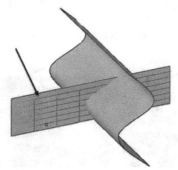

Step 3: Select cutting curves then enter

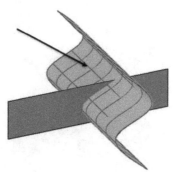

Step 4: Select area to trim

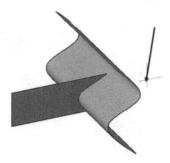

Surface Fillet

Step 1: Ribbon ▶ Surface ▶ Edit ▶ Fillet

Step 2: Select first surface

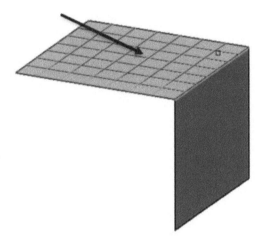

Step 3: Select second surface

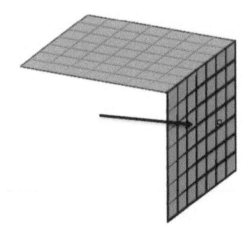

Step 4:- R Enter for radius option.

Step 5: 0.5 Enter for radius then again enter

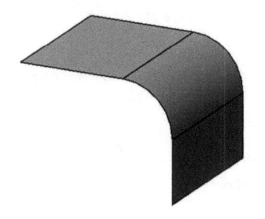

3D Door Creation   CHAPTER-12

3D Door

Step 1: Ribbon ▶ Home tab ▶ Modeling ▶ Extrude

Step 2: Select object then enter

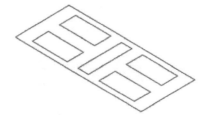

Step 3: 0.1 Enter for extrude height

Step 4: Ribbon Home tab Modeling Presspull

Step 5: Select face

Step 6: 0.2 Enter for height

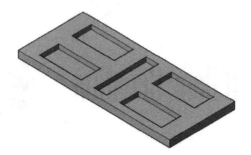

Material

Step 7: MAT Enter for material command

Step 8: Search wood material

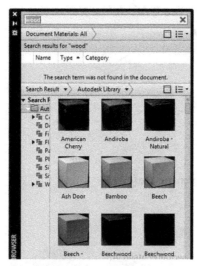

Step 9: Drag and drop material

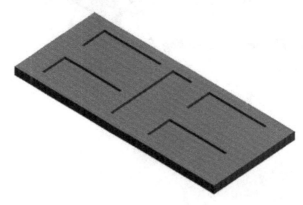

What are the new features introduced in AutoCAD 2017?

CHAPTER-13

Revision Cloud

Step 1: Revcloud Enter

Step 2: Then R enter for rectangle shape of Revision cloud

or

P enter for Polygon shape Revision cloud.

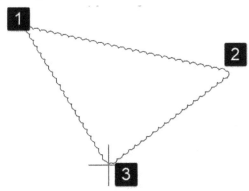

Smart Dimension

In General to measure the diameter of a circle as to measure the length of a line two different tools are required for the same, but with the help of smart dimension's new feature both types of dimension's can be measure with the same tool.

I.e. Smart dimension.

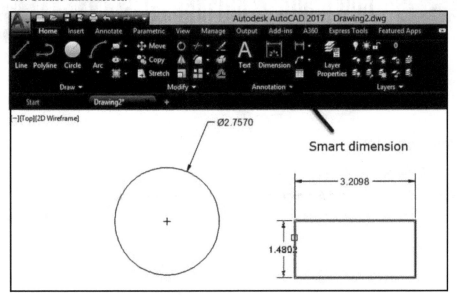

Geometric Center (Osnap)

Geometric any Polygon center point of it is to show. These new features are Object snapping (Osnap).

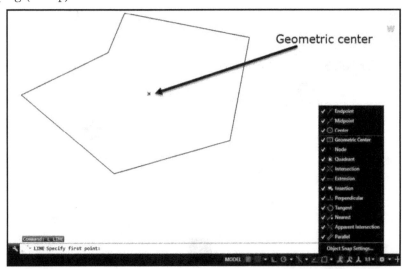

Center Marks and Center Lines

Step 1: Click Annotate tab

Step 2: Click Center lines

Step 3: Select first line

Step 4: Select second line

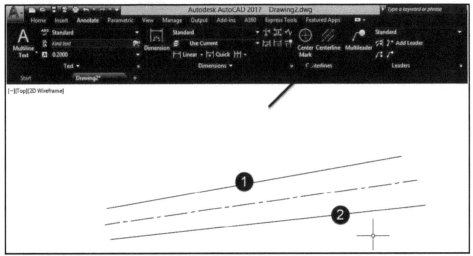

Or

Click center mark then Select circle.

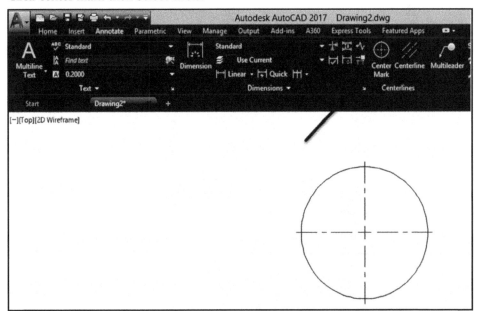

PDF file import

Step 1: Click Insert tab then click Pdf import

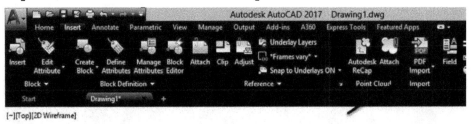

Step 2: Then enter or right click

Step 3: Select file and open

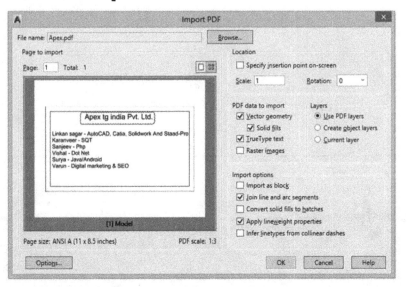

Step 4: Select scale, Rotation angle and ok

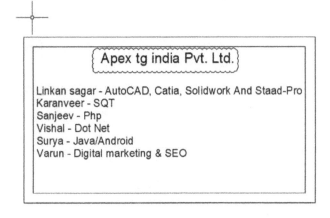

Practice Drawings

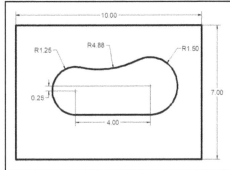

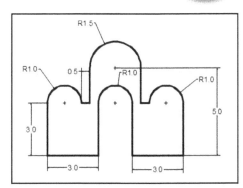

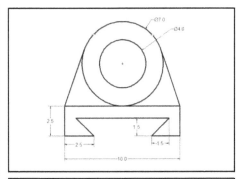

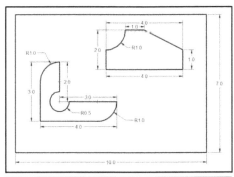

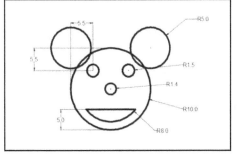

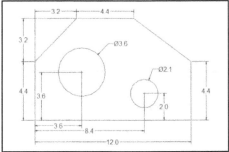

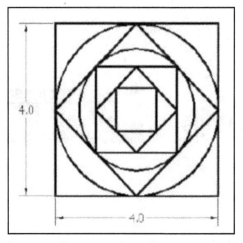

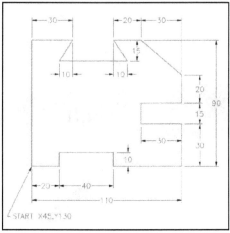

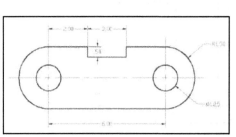

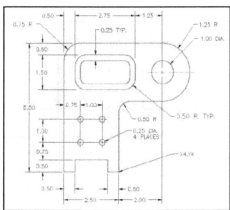

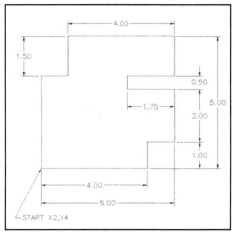

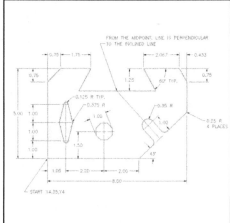

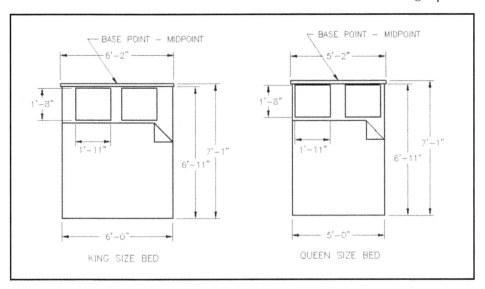

KING SIZE BED

QUEEN SIZE BED

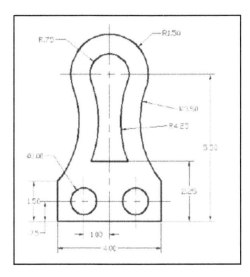

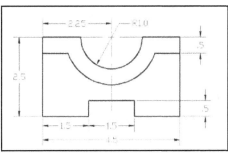

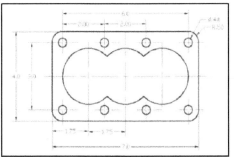

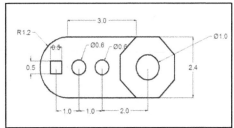

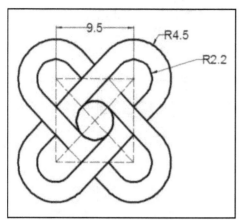

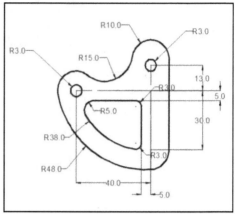

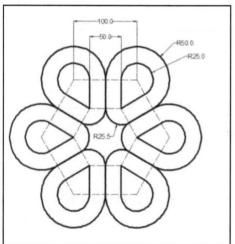

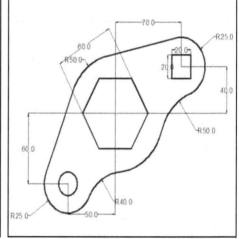

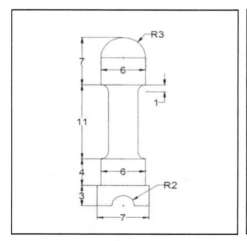

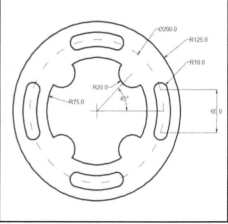

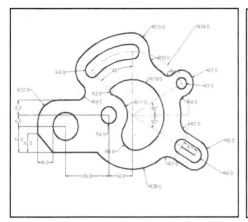

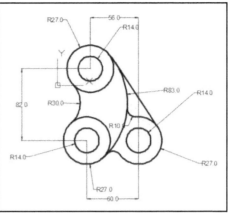

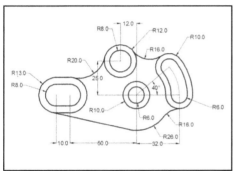

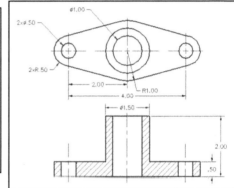

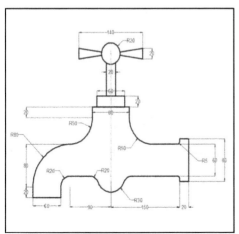

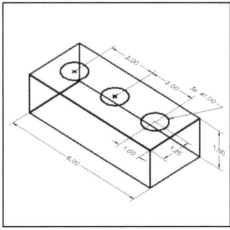

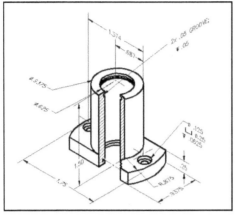

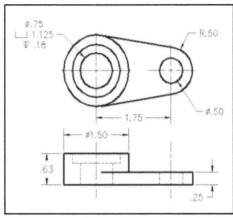

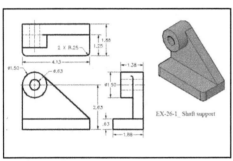

EX-26-1_ Shaft support

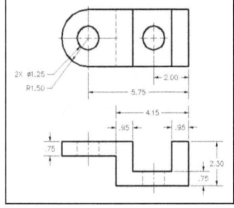

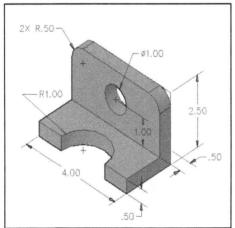

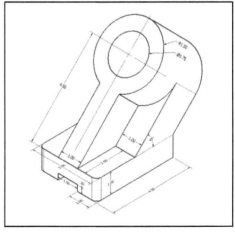

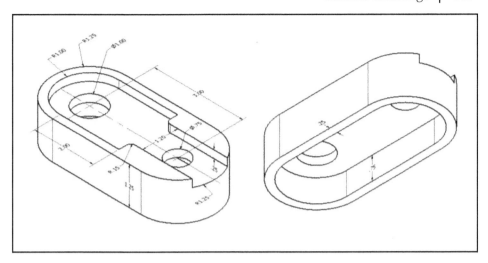

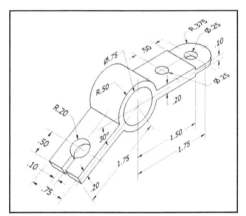

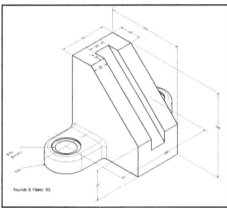

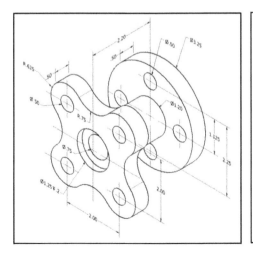

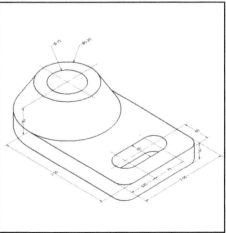

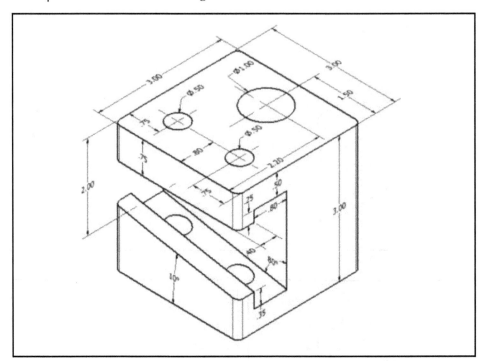

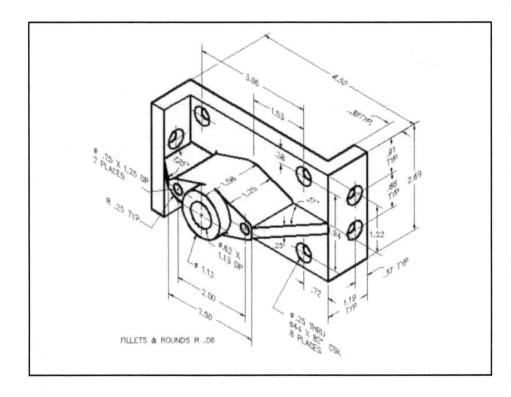

www.ingramcontent.com/pod-product-compliance
Lightning Source LLC
Chambersburg PA
CBHW071215050326
40689CB00011B/2334